FROM PA]
PAU
WITH FO

THE
ARCHIE
MCLEAN
STORY

The man who changed the way Brazilians play football

Foreword by
Chick Young   BBC Scotland

by Peter Cameron

Dedicated to all the Scots and their families who left the Paisley area and went to work for Coats Mill in Sao Paulo, Brazil.

First published in 2007 by Linn Publishers.
(e-mail cath.cameron@ntlworld.com)

ISBN   978-0-9555837-0-4

Printed in Great Britain by Clydeside Press Ltd., Glasgow.

CONTENTS

Acknowledgements

May I take the opportunity to thank a number of people who have given me invaluable help to produce this book. May I thank:

- Jed O'Brien former director of the Scottish Football Museum, who gave me the inspiration and motivation to find out about the life and times of Archie McLean.
- Malcolm McLean, Archie's grandson, for his time, information and photographs and for the tremendous enthusiasm for Archie's life and his football exploits.
- Aiden Hamilton for his book entitled '*An Entirely Different Game*' and for the focus he had in his book on Archie McLean and the chapter on Archie which was called 'Wandered from Scotland'. The book covered the British Influence on Brazilian football. Aiden has a tremendous knowledge and interest on Archie McLean and particularly his football life.
- Richard McBrearty, creator of the Scottish Football Museum at Hampden Park, for his assistance and for his input in setting up the displays on Archie McLean at the museum in Paisley.
- David Roberts of Paisley Museum for the information on this exhibition held at the museum for Archie McLean.
- Amanda Russell and STV for their permission to

include a transcript of the programme on Archie which was shown in May 2006, entitled: Archie McLean *The Forgotten Father of Brazilian Football.*

- Derek Parker of The Paisley Daily Express for his advice and direction.
- John Mills, the Curator of The Sao Paulo Athletics Club, for invaluable information which I could only have obtained from a source such as John, and also for photographs on the Sao Paulo Athletics Club.
- Mara Gago of the British and Commonwealth Community Council of Sao Paulo for the excellent photographs provided for the book.
- Chick Young of BBC Radio Scotland for writing a foreword to the book and for all his enthusiasm for all things pertaining to Paisley and St Mirren.
- Nancy Watson (nee McNeil) for the photographs she provided and her input on 'Uncle Archie' and the Coats Sao Paulo Community.
- The Paisley Sao Paulo group as I refer to them, former employees of Coats who spent years in Sao Paulo who were willing to talk about their experiences in Brazil and their recollections of Archie McLean but did not want to have a mention.
- Lisa Currie of Renfrewshire Council for voluntary services for typing the manuscript for the book.
- May I thank members of my family for their support, encouragement and assistance, especially my wife Cathie Cameron, my daughter Claire Wadsworth and my sister Mairi Hayward.

Foreword

By Chick Young
Of
BBC Scotland

My first match. I can see it now, me and my best buddy
Mel reaching the top of the terracing steps and gazing
down on the promised land. And I'll tell you this, no loss
of any kind of virginity since has thrilled me so. Nor, for
that matter, lasted as long

It was colour all right. The lush green and the bright red of
the Hi Hi jerseys – v-neck and logo-free as all great strips
should be - all in stark contrast to the grainy black and
white pictures on the little television that sat in the corner
of our living room.

Until I went to a game I kind of assumed that Scottish
football was grey with horizontal lines. It might even have
come with a vertical hold.

Frankly I don't ever remember not being truly, madly in
love with football. It consumed me as a kid and I
desperately wanted to make it my life. I dreamt of playing
at the very top until it slowly dawned on me that I was
lacking in one pretty essential factor. Ability.

Still, Plan B has served me well, nearly four decades now
of modest income writing and broadcasting about the

wacky world of the Scottish game.

I love people who share my passion. Who respect that the history of football in this country is just as important as its present and its past.

That without acknowledging those who blazed a trail and toasting their memory there is no real hope in understanding what the game stands for in Scotland.

Archie McLean is part of that story.

The world is shrinking. Once upon a time my dear old mum would take me to Millport, as glorious a spot with which God ever blessed the earth. We might as well have been travelling to the other end of the solar system.

Now I toddle down the brae leading to Largs with a sense of voyage the equivalent of which once was the length of our hall.

Imagine though when Archie McLean left these shores for Brazil. CalMac don't do Sao Paulo.

It was a long way and a long time ago.

But bless his love of the game and bless his sense of adventure. And most of all bless his devilish spirit and his eagerness to teach our sport to the Brazilians who would come back and show what brilliant pupils they had become.

Peter Cameron, in writing this book, has played his part in preserving the memory of an Archie who was performing miracles in South America decades before his namesake Gemmill – another St Mirren man as it happens – was scoring Scotland's greatest ever goal in Argentina.

It's a hell of a tale. Of travel, of adventure, of life. But most of all about the fact that McLean loved a right good kick at the ball. Whether he was in Barrhead or Brazil.

In the end he couldn't, for all the magic of that wondrous land, resist coming home to spend the autumn of his life watching the Saints at Love Street. This too I understand.

Paul Simon once implored us to preserve our memories. "They're all that's left you," he suggested.

Actually the game of football has a future too. But for all that, the advice of the song writer is sound.

Preface

I have always loved football as long as I can remember, 1953 was a significant year in my becoming aware of the beautiful game. I recall the anticipation of listening on Saturday 18th April to the Scottish Home Service of the BBC radio to the England V Scotland international from Wembley Stadium.

The commentators were Raymond Glendenning and Peter Thomson. Coverage started at 2.55pm, five minutes before the game kicked off. No two hours of build up as it is in the Twentieth First century. The contrast between the two commentators could have not been greater, which outlined in a way the difference between the English and Scots as nations. I recall the excitement the commentators brought to the game and how although at the time I had not seen a professional game, they painted such vivid word pictures that I felt I was there at the game. Along with Peter Thomson was another radio commentator George Davidson whose style and delivery were very different from Peter's but just as exciting and made games live for me.

The result was a two all draw with the Scottish centre forward Laurie Reilly scoring twice.

The Scottish team was:

G.Farm, G.Young, S.Cox, J.G. Louden, F.Brennan, D.Cowie, T.Wright, R.Johnstone, L.Reilly, W.Steel and W.Liddell with the crowd at the game being 97,000.

Later in the day at 6.20pm the Scottish Home Service had a programme of sports results followed at 6.28pm by Sports Reel with a sound picture from the commentary recorded during the England and Scottish International at Wembley and reports from 'A and B' division games.

The programme was arranged by Peter Thomson who was having a busy day that day; the programme was followed by an half hour of Scottish dance music played by Jimmy Shand and his band.

Apart from the now familiar 'Phone ins' which are part of the Twentieth First century, the schedule has not changed a lot since 1953, on Saturday early evening radio. I recall my Dad always went to visit his friend Peter, the local village barber and they would listen to Sportsround and debate the talking points of the day.

1954 was an exciting year, as I went with my Dad to my first professional game in Inverness at the home of Clacknacuddan who were playing their great rivals Inverness Thistle. It was a game between what locals referred to as Clack V Thistle on 23rd October 1954 in the fourth round of the Scottish Cup.

Clacknacuddan had won through to this fourth round with replays over Elgin City and Berwick Rangers, so the scene was set for this Cup game. I was excited and was a supporter of Clach that day but 'my team' lost out two-one to Thistle. It was a great day when I was able to realise a dream of seeing a football match rather than just listening to the radio commentary.

In 1958 the World Cup was held in Sweden. I watched the game with my Dad and a friend, and we watched the final seeing Brazil win 5-2 over Sweden with a team which included Garringa and Pele who scored two goals in the final and six in the tournament. The Brazilians played a formation of 4-2-4, not that I was aware of that at the time. On 11th May 2001 at the Walker Halls in Troon, I heard a lecture given by Jed O'Brien (Jed was at that time Director of The Scottish Football Museum) on the theme 'Football, the game Scotland gave the world.' He talked about the influence of Scottish football in Brazil, he referred to Aiden Hamilton's book , 'An Entirely Different Game', and talked about the chapter in the book entitled 'The Wanderer from Scotland'which discussed the influence on Brazilian Football of an Archie McLean. Jed gave out a handout on which he outlined various significant events from 1872 to the time of his presentation in 2001. He indicated that in 1909, Archie McLean moved from Ayr to Brazil (via Paisley); in fact the date Archie went to Brazil was 1912 from Johnstone.

On Saturday 3rd September 2005, the crowd was gathering for the late afternoon kick off in the World Cup qualifying game between Scotland and Italy at the Scotland National Stadium, Hampden Park in Glasgow.

Among the various street traders and musicians outside the stadium was a Samba band. The Samba band was a Scottish Samba band which went by the name of 'Samba Ya Bamba'. Their presence and music added to the atmosphere of the occasion. What place did the Samba Ya Bamba band have at this very Scottish event and why should we focus on a band member playing? All will be revealed as the story unfolds . Over not just past years, but past centuries, Scotland and its people made great contributions all over the world. Often those who have left Scotland for other places have had their talents and input recognised and they were revered in a way which would not have happened to them back in Bonnie Scotland. This is one such story.   Johnstone 2007

Introduction

I have always had a fascination for Brazil. Rio and Sao Paulo have always appeared to be exciting cities.

I never met Archie Fulton McLean, but I have learned of his life and the person he was. He was a real gentleman and a great guy. The fact is, that for almost 100 years there have been press articles about him, his life as a footballer, and his lasting legacy to Brazilian football.

The story begins with the Miller family in Fairlie, a small village in Ayrshire, John Miller, like so many Scots over the years, moved abroad in order to find the opportunities which did not exist in Scotland, in the 19th century. John's son, Charles, was the 'Father of Brazilian football', and was able to be part of setting up organised competition football in the Sao Paulo area. With his arrival in Brazil, Archie McLean was able to be part of building on what had been established.

Included in this book has been the social history of Paisley, as the town was in the early 20th century of the development of Coats Mills, in Paisley on a local basis, Paisley as well as on the world wide stage, with detailed descriptions of the major development of the Coats Mills in Sao Paulo.

It is remarkable that three men, with a Scots background, were major influences in the tremendous development of football, in both Brazil and Argentina. The ultimate achievement from these beginnings was the 'Beautiful Team' winning the 1970 World Cup in Mexico, for Brazil.

The Scottish Football Museum was set up, and within the museum, the Scottish Hall of Fame and the Role of Honour were established. It is here that those whose talents have graced the Scottish National Team over the years, are recognised.

The Paisley Museum, in conjunction with the Scottish Football Museum, worked together to honour Archie McLean. Maybe such an event would never have happened without the Football Museum.

Professionalism, has been a subject of debate in football, as in other sports. The 'Corinthian Spirit', playing for the love of the sport, has in football become a thing of the past, at a top level, anyway. Charles Miller and Archie McLean could have taught our overpaid professional football players of the 21st Century about the spirit of 'Playing the Game.'

When Scotland played Georgia in March 2007, in Hampden Park, a Samba Band entertained the crowd, having graduated from playing outside the stadium . A member of the band was Malcolm McLean, Archie's grandson who was born in Brazil. So at last a McLean played at Hampden, if not for Scotland, for the Scottish fans at a full house of 50,000 spectators.

Outside the entrance to The Scottish Football Museum there is a notice which makes the following statement. 'Football has evolved from being a recreational pastime into the world's most popular sport. Scotland has had a pre-eminent role in the early development of football and Scots players, managers and coaches have played a master part in the process of the game both in Scotland, throughout the United Kingdom and abroad. 'From Paisley to Paulo with football. The Archie McLean story – the Man who changed the way the Brazilians play football'. This book amply confirms the statement.

Introduction to Chapters One to Three
Before telling the Archie McLean Story the first three chapters of this book set the scene.

Chapter One - Tells how football came to Brazil and the role Charles Miller played in establishing the game in the Sao Paulo area before Archie McLean's arrival.

Chapter Two - A picture has been painted of what Paisley, Archie's home town was like at the turn of the twentieth century. Where he worked prior to going to Sao Paulo.

Chapter Three - Gives the history of Coats Mills who were Archie McLean's employers for the main part of his working life .

ONE

The Man who 'invented' Football

Charles Miller brought football to Brazil and his background was Scottish. John, Charles Miller's father was born in Fairlie, a small seaside village on the Ayrshire coast. John was born in Burnfoot house in Fairlie, in 1844 to Andrew and Elizabeth Miller, one of four children. Burnfoot house is in a lovely location in the village of Fairlie. At the bottom of the garden there runs a burn in which small trout swim to get to the sea. It must have been a joy for John to spend part of his childhood there. He would have looked back at later times in his life in Brazil, and thought of the summers he spent in Fairlie, and the freedom he had as he played in the burn at the back of Burnfoot house. Andrew's family had to share the house with five other families, each family having two rooms, one to eat in and the other for sleeping.

John Miller was tall and handsome, and by virtue of his Scottish upbringing and the family's association with the Free Church of Scotland which was as formed a break away from the Church of Scotland, he possessed qualities which allowed him to take advantage of the opportunities of the age he lived in. Andrew and the family later moved to Greenock to Lyndock Street, to take up residence in one of the tenement buildings there. Andrew found employment as a Porter at the docks.

John Miller was an engineer and decided to emigrate to Brazil where his skills were much sought after in the emerging economy . He went to work with the Sao Paulo Railway Company, which operated from Sao Paulo to Santos, providing transport for coffee to the coast. John married Carlota Alexandra Fox, who was Brazilian, but had English ancestors. The couple's second son Charles William Miller was born in Sao Paulo on 24 November 1874.

At the age of nine, Charles was sent to boarding school in England. In 1884 he sailed for Southhampton, with his brother John, and his cousin William Fox Rule. They sailed on the 'SS Elbe', arriving in Southhampton at the end of July. His new home was 'Bannister Court' a boarding school, and of the new experiences that Charles was able to enjoy, none was more exciting than to witness his first game of Association Football, which he found fascinating.

At that time, the question of Amateurism V Professionalism was a divisive issue. In later life Charles was to come face to face with this in Sao Paulo. From his time at Bannister Court, he held a strong belief that football was, and always should be, a 'mere pastime' played for enjoyment, and never for money.

During Charles Miller's ten years at Bannister Court, his main passion was for football, and he endeavoured to use his energies and talents to play in every position in a football team. He played regularly for the school's team from the time he was fourteen in their red and black colours. He was given the opportunity to play in various positions before settling to play on the left wing.

Having completed his schooling in Southhampton,

Charles Miller sailed back to Brazil on the 'Magdelena', and arrived at Santos in November 1894. This was the moment that Brazilian football began, when Charles Miller arrived on the quay at Santos with a leather football under each arm. He also brought with him a pump, a pair of boots, and most importantly a book of rules. In essence, those football related items were his degree and he had graduated in football. When the Brazilian Football Association came to celebrate their centenary, the celebrations took place one hundred years to the day that Charles arrived at Santos.

Charles was met by his mother, and they travelled by the railway to Sao Paulo, with his mother updating him on what happened in the family in the ten years he had been in England. They arrived at Luz station, a local landmark, and a hub of activities in this fast growing city.

Charles was anxious to play football, but soon realised that no one played football in Brazil. He encountered lots of negative attitudes towards why football could not be played in Brazil, and anyway the cricket season was in full swing. Charles discovered the Sao Paulo Athletics Club, which the English speakers referred to as 'spack'. His family had started and administered the club. It would play an important part in Charles's life over the years to come.

The Sao Paulo Athletics Club (SPAC) was formed in 1888 by the British living in Sao Paulo by way of having a sports club. The club became for the British community the centre of their social life. Among the many things the SPAC was known for was that from 1888 onwards, a visitor could always be served a proper pot of tea. No sooner had the club been established, than cricket matches were being arranged with other British communities in other parts of South America, both near and far. Among the founders of the club were several close relatives of Charles Miller. In 1897 the SPAC moved to its new home, the home it still has in the twenty first century, and by 1906 the club was able to purchase the land.

In the ten years Charles was away, Sao Paulo had grown by five times to a population nearing 200,000 by 1905. When Charles arrived back in Sao Paulo, the cricket season was in full swing. Charles was anxious to introduce football to the locals and picked two teams to try out what he referred to as his 'Neat Little Game'.

The game was to take place on Sunday at 4pm, and Charles was excited, only to be let down when not one of those invited turned up.

Slowly Charles managed to persuade a number of his friends and acquaintances to join him to play football. Finally a proper game was arranged between Sao Paulo Railway and The Gas Works. Charles, although he had no direct association with either team, played centre forward for the Railway Team, he was their captain and also referee. Before the game got underway, Charles had to hold up a flap of sewn leather which he brought back from England and pumped air into it.

Despite playing for one of the teams, no-one had any concerns about him being the referee. The game was played on Sunday 19th April 1895, and Sao Paulo Railway won 4-2. This may not have been the first game played in Brazil, but it was a significant event. Football (there was no equivalent Portuguese word) played by Association Rules had arrived in Brazil. Football had arrived, and was a success, all due to Charles Miller's efforts and this in only a few short months since arriving in Sao Paulo.

In 1896 another significant event took place in the development of football in Sao Paulo, when Augustus Shaw arrived at Santos with a Bible and a deflated leather ball. He was on his way to teach at the Mackenzie College in Sao Paulo. Unlike Charles Miller, the ball Augustus brought was a basketball , and he quickly went to work to introduce the students who were mainly Brazilian and Catholic, to basketball and its thirteen rules. However, instead of using their hands the students used their feet much to Shaw's disdain. From these developments, Shaw realised that football was the game the students wanted to play.

James Naismith, a Canadian of Scottish parents had invented basketball in the winter of 1891/92 while James was a teacher in the YMCA College in Massachusetts. Naismith's Scottish connection doesn't seem so widely known and it is another opportunity to praise those of Scottish ancestry, and their world wide contributions to so many aspects of life.

In 1898 Hans Nobiling arrived in Sao Paulo from Hamburg. He tried to involve his friends in football, but they viewed the game as being the 'English Disease' and did not want to be involved. He tried to get involved with the SPAC, and quickly came to realise that if he as a German wanted to be part of a football team in Sao Paulo, he had better start his own team. Nobiling formed a team with young men of various nationalities who would use two languages, English for football and Portuguese for general chat on the field. There were now three football teams in Sao Paulo: Sao Paulo Athletics Club (SPAC), Mackenzie College and Hans Nobiling's team, but a competitive match among these three teams had not taken place. On 5th March 1899, the first game of football involving two teams from Sao Paulo took place between Hans Nobiling's multi-national team and Mackenzie College, composed mainly of Brazilians. The game ended in a 0-0 draw, which was no more than a starting point for competitive football in Brazil. This spurred Charles Miller to get involved, and a week after the first game, SPAC beat Mackenzie College 3-0.

Hans Nobiling then decided to persuade his fellow Germans to set up a club in Sao Paulo, and the team was called Sport Club Germania. Nobiling's old team became Sport Club Internationale.

A group of young Brazilians formed another team and called themselves Club Athletico Paulistano. The name was shortened to Paulistano or CAP. The team received permission to use the cycling ground, the Velodromo, to play their home games.

Internationale's new captain replacing Hans Nobiling was a Brazilian named Antonia Casimiro da Costa, who organised these five teams in the first competitive league in Brazil. Antonia was frustrated at how long it took for footballs to be shipped from Southampton, and approached a local shoemaker, who was able to make a football in Sao Paulo, thus starting a profitable new business.

In season 1905, a sixth team was admitted to the Liga. This team was formed from Paulistano who had too many players. The new team had the name Associaca Athletica Das Palmaeiras and finished bottom of the league. That season, SPAC beat Paulistano in a play off for the Silver Trophy on the last Sunday in October 1905. This was the third year SPAC had won the league and were able to keep the cup. Paulistano were unhappy about some aspects of the final match and resigned from the Liga.

At the end of 1905, Paulistano rejoined the Liga and the owners of the Velodromo demolished that stadium and built a brand new stadium.

The 1906 season began in May, and Charles Miller and SPAC were having a disastrous season. Miller had fallen in love with his cousin Antonietta Rudge, who was English on her father's side and Portuguese on her mother's side. Antonietta was the fifth of sixteen children. Born in 1885, she was artistic and had different interests from Charles. They had married in early 1906, and in that season Charles and SPAC lost the place, finishing bottom of the Liga. Charles resigned before the new season started in 1907.

Charles Miller was an amateur and played football for the love of the game. Imagine his consternation in season 1910, when the Club Athletico Paulistano employed a professional, Jock Hamilton who played for Fulham. This move helped Paulistano to win the Liga that year, and money became part of the football setup in Sao Paulo. Payments were first made to trainers and then to players. That year SPAC were bottom of the Liga.

Of Charles Miller, Thomas Mazzoni wrote at a much later date, 'Charles had youthful enthusiasm, his cordial amateurism and his sporting spirit prevailing in all of his attitudes'.

Charles was an excellent referee and had the respect of all players who observed his fairness and impartiality. In 1902, Charles was able to obtain from England a book entitled 'Referees Chart'. At the time, the policy was that Paulista referees were players of the clubs which were not involved in a particular game. At various times in his football career, Charles received praise for his contribution and personal qualities. He left to return to Sao Paulo from Southampton. At a meeting of the Hampshire County Football Association, the following comment was made 'a more popular and genuine player than Miller could not be imagined'.

Besides Charles Miller who was a missionary and introducer, two other men had a major influence in the formation of the Paulista League. Hans Nobling was the socialiser of the sport, the third was Antonia Casimiro da Costa', a Brazilian who was the idealiser of the first football league in Brazil.

On the 29 June 1899 which was a holiday to celebrate Saint Peter and Saint Paul, the Patrons of the City of Sao Paulo, the Sao Paulo Athletics Club accepted a challenge to play Hans Nobiling's Team. The attendance was sixty, and SPAC won 1 - 0, and of course Charles Miller played his part.

The Club House of SPAC was located in the Consolacao district of Sao Paulo. At the end of Season

1903, SPAC had won the 'Antonio Casimiro da Costa' silver cup and Charles Miller had refereed more games than anyone else. At the end of Season 1904, SPAC won the cup again, and the celebration focused on Charles Miller's contribution with the victorious team singing to Miller 'for he's a jolly good fellow'. SPAC were able to keep the cup, after their third win. SPAC had rented their ground since 1899 and were able in 1906 to purchase the ground which is now known as Rua Visconde de Quro Preto.

A new cup was played for in the League from season 1905, and came to be known as the 'Count Penteado' Cup and was won as follows:-

1905 – Paulistano
1906 – Germania
1907 – International
1908 – Paulistano
1909 – A A Palmeiras
1910 – A A Palmeiras
1911 - SPAC

In 1911 SPAC won the cup, but Palmeiras refused to hand over the trophy. This was the last year SPAC won the league. By the season 1911, Charles Miller had officially stopped playing .

Among the areas of difference between the clubs, was that of professionalism, which had been developing since the season of 1908. This led SPAC to leave the league in 1912season . SPAC was a club that was formed in 1888, on the basis of sport being played for its own sake and not for money.

Other changes were taking place in Brazil, and in the Sao Paulo area in particular. Brazil had embraced football rather than basketball. The country had chosen cars in preference to railways, and during Charles Miller's life, Sao Paulo had become a great industrial city, the biggest in Brazil. This growth seemed to be never ending and caused the British community to wonder what their long term place in this growth would be.

Charles Miller prospered, and was able to build a large villa on Rua Mexico in a very pleasant part of town, where he lived with his wife Antonietta and their children Carlos and Helena. Charles worked for the Royal Mail and by now he refereed football rather than playing, and watched SPAC's matches with enthusiasm.

In Brazil, football was referred to as 'Futebol', and had a definite national focus. Brazilian players were creating a game based on artistry rather than regimentation. Players were being paid, and teams in the 1920's had players from all ethnic backgrounds.

As with so much on the initial development of football in Brazil, Charles Miller was involved in the first international played in Brazil. It was against South Africa and Charles played in the game. The results were a 6-0 victory for South Africa, the game being played in Sao Paulo in 1902.

It wasn't till 1912 that the first game was played by a Brazilian Team in the now familiar green and yellow colours. The game was against Exeter City, who were on a tour of Brazil. The game was played in Rio at the Fluminense Football Clubs ground, and the 'Brasileiros' as they were referred to, won 2-0.

As a follow up at the beginning of 1913, the first official international involving a Brazilian National Team was played against Argentina with a 1-0 win.

Arthur Anderson who was co founder of the Peninsular Steam Navigation Steam co. later know as P.O was anxious to start a school for the sons of his captains. He appointed the Reverend George Ellaby to be the headmaster and to move to Bannister college in Southhampton. During the time Charles Miller spent at Bannister Court, he lost his father , his sister and two brothers, and came to rely on the Ellaby family for support during these challenging times. The school was founded in 1884, and Charles, his brother John and cousin William Fox Rule were among the first year's intake.

Charles wrote to the Reverend Ellaby at the beginning of 1904, ten years after his return to Sao Paulo, and outlined his sporting activities as follows :

'Now as to Sports, which will no doubt interest you most, with cricket we have not been able to do very much except among the English. We have a nice ground, pavilion, three tennis courts which most clubs in England would be proud of.

Now we shall speak about football, you will be surprised to hear that football is the game here. There are seventy clubs in the city of Sao Paulo. Two years ago a Brazilian named Antonio and myself formed a league. We get two or three thousand fans at a match but at the final, six thousand attended.

A week ago I was asked to referee a match with twenty small boys on each side they played for two and a half hours and the youngsters hardly spoke a word during the game, about fifteen hundred people turned up to watch the game. No less than two thousand footballs have been sold here within the last twelve months and nearly every village has a team now.'

In his business Charles joined with Edward Goddard, and rented offices in Praca Da Republica in the centre of Sao Paulo. They started their own Travel Agency, and soon three generations of Charles's family worked for the firm, as his son Carlos and his granddaughter Therezina joined the Miller Goddard company.

When Carlos Miller's wife died, he moved himself and his three children into Charles' home. By now Charles was in his late seventies and in failing health. His granddaughter Therezina found Charles lying unconscious, late in June 1953, and he passed away in hospital on June 30th 1953.

The funeral took place on the afternoon of July 1st, and a football match was in progress at the Pacaembu stadium. As a mark of respect and the affection which the football world in Sao Paulo still had for Charles Miller, as his cortege passed the stadium, the referee stopped the game. The players and spectators stood in silence till the hearse had passed, on its way to the cemetery.

This old cemetery is in the old centre of Sao Paulo, and Charles was buried alongside his mother, his sister and two brothers in the family's plot.

Looking at the names on the gravestone in the

Protestant cemetery, one could imagine being in Scotland, with such names as Anderson, Campbell, Hunter, Scott and Wilson appearing on the stones. The Miller plot is impressive, with various stones and crosses. There lay all direct family members and cousins who had passed on in this foreign part.

Of the teams that played in the Liga Paulista in its first season in the eighteen nineties, SPAC is now called Club Athletico Sao Paulo, Mackenzie College has very tenacious Presbyterians connections in the twenty first century and is a large university.

The Club Athletico Paulistano, as it was 100 years ago, is a private sports club. In another part of Sao Paulo the Esporte Club Pinheros is another exclusive club, and all have remained amateur clubs.

Charles had a park named after him, Praca Charles Miller, where on match days the local Corinthians play in black and white. They have had on their team sheet over the years such famous World Cup stars as Socrates, Rivelino,Gilmar, Rivaldo, Dida and Edilson. In a town called Balua, there is a bar called Charles Miller. Although those in the bar have no idea who Charles Miller was, one local taxi driver volunteered the information, that Charles Miller was the one who 'invented football'.

TWO
Paisley in the Early Twentieth Century

In Scotland every village, town or city has a meeting point, and Paisley is no exception. Paisley Cross, which is at the corner of High Street and Moss Street, is that part of Paisley.

Paisley Cross has not really altered since the creation of Paisley as a Burgh 1488. The Cross has always been a gathering place in times of sadness or celebration.

In the early twentieth century, households did not have fridges or freezer, so the townsfolk had to shop daily. Horse and carts were a feature of the Paisley streets as they delivered groceries and bread. These businesses were owned and run by local families. There were a number of bakeries where bread was baked three times a day and would always be on sale and freshly baked.

The local football team in Paisley is called St Mirren - as it is in the twenty-first century, and was in the early twentieth century. St Mirren was a founder member of the Scottish Football League, and was formed way back in 1877. In the 1900's, the team attracted crowds of 20,000, compared with 3,000 in the early 21st century.

At that time there was no television. Many of those in employment, worked for long hours, often in unpleasant working conditions. When people could, they used the little free time that they had, to get outdoors to engage in such activities as rowing, rambling, bowling, cycling, curling and running.

One special day in the 1900's was the Sma' Shot Day

holiday. This holiday had its history in Weavers and Unions against the 'Cork ' , the man who paid the weavers. This holiday, was unique to Paisley, and held on the first Saturday in July, and recently has been revived to be held in the Paisley Town Centre. The celebration often involved those having the holiday to go by train or bus on an outing to the coast (the Clyde Coast) .

In 1905 the Royal Alexandra Infirmary was opened. The infirmary came about, as a result of great fundraising events and contributions by the Coat's family, who owned the local mills.

One of the outdoor activities in which the men of Paisley participated during the summer months, was bowling on grass. All who played, had to dress very formally, with suits, shirts, ties and hats or caps. In those days, no women could play, but could spectate.

The people of Paisley would dress very formally when playing bowls, and for activities, such as church outings, which were very popular in the early 20th century. To the south of the town were the Gleniffer Braes which weren't too far and a popular location for such outings.

One of the many dairies in the town was the Craigielea dairy, a small family business. Dairies in Paisley like the Craigielea Dairy had a byre in the back of the premises, where the cows belonging to the dairy would be milked, giving really fresh milk.

A feature of the centre of Paisley was the narrow streets, some of which were widened in the twentieth century. As part of this process it had been intended to widen the High Street, but funding wasn't available, so in the twenty-first century, most of Victorian High Street of Paisley is still as it was a hundred years ago.

In order to shoe all the horses that 'tood and flaud' the streets of Paisley, there were many small blacksmiths shops, known locally as 'smiddies' which were a feature of the working life of the town.

One of the features of life in Paisley at the turn of the century was that there was lots of employment in the area. This work was neither well paid nor often very safe and not just for the young.

It was a labour intensive society where they worked in the mills, in the factories, in the shops (there were no supermarkets then).

There were also no state pensions or a retirement age, so many men and women worked till old age. Industry was at the heart of Paisley, Scotland's largest town, with such well known names as Brown & Polson's Cornflour, Robertson's Jam, and Coats and Clark the thread makers, being the main employers. Thread makers dominated the industrial life of the town, and employed 10,000 workers, the majority of whom were women. Other industries, such as shipbuilding and engineering, were also an important part of what allowed Paisley, at that time, to be a busy and thriving town.

THREE

The Mills in Paisley and Beyond

In the late eighteenth Century, the brothers Peter and James Clark worked independently, as manufacturers of twine for heddles, and as weavers' furnishers, providing the weaving trade with items such as reeds and shuttles.

Around 1806, the weaving business was hit by Napoleon's Berlin Decree, banning exports to Great Britain. This situation prompted Peter Clark to experiment in producing heddles of cotton instead of silk - the embryo of what was to become the successful business of the Clark family, who began manufacturing cotton thread on the north side of the River Cart, close to the Hammils in Paisley in 1812. In the early days, thread would be wound on pirns for the price of five pence, which was redeemable on the return of the empty pirn.

In 1819, the elder James Clark retired, and he sold the business to his sons James Junior and John. Together, they formed the company of J & J Clark, and worked hard to build a profitable business. They retired in 1852, and the business was left in the hands of James Clark of Ralston, the son of John. Expanding rapidly, it was necessary to employ his brothers John and Stewart, to assist him.

Other branches of the Clark family set up thread companies in Paisley, and in a relatively short time, amalgamated with Clark & Co. These included Kerr & Co of Underwood, Carlisle and John Clark junior of Well Street. The Counting House of the latter can still be seen at the corner of Well Street and Clavering Street, recognised by the '£' sign visible on the stonework. This was a time of great expansion, and by 1880, Anchor Mills was running over 230,000 spindles, and employing over 3,500 workers, who were producing about 15 tons of finished goods each day.

In 1802, James Coats, having recently returned from service with the Ayrshire Fencibles, set up business in the weaving trade. Shortly afterwards, he went into partnership with James Whyte, producing Canton Crepe shawls, in which the skill of yarn twisting was an integral part.

In 1826, James Coats built a small thread factory behind his house, Back Row, Ferguslie, now known as Maxwellton Road in Paisley. It was a three flatted building, powered by a single 12hp engine.

In 1830. James retired. His Shawl Factory was taken over by his son William, and the thread business was passed to sons James and Peter, but they had to pay their father a rent of £500 per annum. On 1 July 1830, J & P Coats was formed, and shortly afterwards, their brother Thomas joined the partnership. By 1840, hard work had increased the trade, and consequently, the size of the factory. New engines, which gave out 50hp were installed.

1845 saw the death of James, leaving Peter and Thomas to carry on the business. In that year, a further 3 acres was acquired at Ferguslie, where No.2 Mill was built.

Steady expansion took place over the years, and in 1887, a Half-timers School was built. The school allowed the children aged between 10 and 13 years to go to school for half the day, and work in the factory for the other half. Also built was a Glazing and Polishing Mill, which was the No. 1 Spinning Mill and the 'piece de resistance'. Such a notable building it was, that "The Architect" publication gave over their middle page spread to the acclaim of this building. It was a huge building, which housed all processes involved in the spinning of yarn from raw cotton. The machinery was powered by two Compound Tandem engines, producing 2,000hp, with a flywheel 35ft in diameter.

1890 saw yet another imposing building added to the Ferguslie complex, in that of No. 8 Twisting Mill. Four years later, the Dyeworks and No. 9 Twisting Mill were erected.

J & P Coats became a Public Company in 1890, declaring a capital of £5,750,000, the largest ever known at that time, for such a company.

By the 1880's, a difficult situation had developed. Both Coats' and Clark's firms had grown so large, that competition for a limited market grew fierce. Each had announced large price reductions to attract custom.

However, early in 1889, an amicable agreement was reached between the firms, and an office was rented in St Mirren Street in Paisley, where their representatives could discuss joint interests. An agreement was formalised in 1890, when the Central Agency was established to represent the interests of Clark & Co, J & P Coats Limited, and the English firm of Jonas Brook & Bros of Huddersfield.

A piece of ground was purchased in Bothwell Street

Glasgow, where an office was built for the Central Agency and opened in 1893. It was large enough to accommodate a staff of 300.

The Central Agency arrangement worked so well for the Companies, that in April 1896, it was announced that Clark & Co and J & P Coats Limited were to amalgamate under the Coats name. In May of that year, Brook Bros were also absorbed into the newly strengthened Company, and in June, negotiations began with Chadwick & Bros of Bolton. By July, the new combine was the largest thread firm in the world.

The Mile End Mill on the Anchor Mill site, at the East end of Paisley, was built in 1898 for twisting processes. This was an impressive six storey building with its adjacent engine house and boiler house. In the Twenty First Century, the building still stands. It houses various businesses, a local college and houses the Mill Museum. At the Ferguslie Mills the famous Turkey Red Dyeing was introduced, and a building for this purpose was completed in 1901. By 1904, 10,000 workers were employed in the Paisley Mills.

The engines which operated the machine by a rope drive required 400 tons of coal per day. The engine houses were immaculate, and furbished in a style befitting a ballroom.

Kilnside House, which had been the home of the Stewart Clark family, became part of Anchor Mills in 1911. It was used as a canteen, and when the extension was built in 1916, it could seat 800 of the workforce at one time. It was sold in 1985, and became a snooker club. It was mysteriously razed to the ground by fire in the mid-1990s. The ground was sold to a developer, and is now home to block of flats.

It is unlikely, that when the Coats and Clarks set up their small businesses in the West and East End of Paisley, they could have foreseen the role their businesses were to play in Paisley, or indeed in the world at large.

The international side of the business began with the exporting of 75% of the Coats' production in the 1830s. As selling difficulties had arisen, lawyer brother Andrew Coats was dispatched to New York in 1839. He found many fraudulent practices going on, and in fact on one particular day, Andrew brought 16 actions of injunction against counterfeiting.

By 1855, George A Clark had set up home in New York, and opened an office in Warren Street. It was George who decided that it would be more prudent to manufacture in the USA. In December 1864, it was announced that a Clarks Mill was to be built at Newark, New Jersey. This mill later became a massive complex. There they produced 6 Cord Spool Cotton, initially labelled "Our New Thread", and later 'ONT'. The success of this thread being produced in the USA, undoubtedly influenced Coats Spool Company to build their Mill at Pawtucket, where the mill grew from small beginnings, to cover 55 acres.

Towards the end of the Twentieth Century, Coats no longer manufactured in Paisley, but they manufactured in 43 countries, employing over 37,000 throughout the world, and in addition, had sales operations in a number of other countries.

Four
Countdown to Consolacao

The Story moves from Sao Paulo in Brazil, to Paisley in Scotland. Paisley the largest town in Scotland, is located a few miles west of Glasgow, Scotland's largest city.

On 11th July 1886, Archibald Fulton McLean was born in Paisley to John McLean ,a threadmill tender and Jane Fulton. They had been married on 31st December 1868. At the time of their marriage, John was a tobacco spinner and Jane a steam-loom lummar.

Archie's Grandfather John McLean was a mill manager and James Fulton a weaver. These occupations gave a picture of the industrial life in Paisley in the 19th Century. By 1891, the family were living in Barclay Street in Paisley, and there were seven children, Archie being the youngest. The 1891 census records that Archie had two older brothers and four older sisters. The children in the McLean family were:

James	19	Threadmill Worker
Janet	17	Threadmill Worker
Jane	14	Threadmill Worker
John	12	Scholar
Elizabeth	10	Scholar
Ester	7	Scholar
Archibald	4	Scholar

So besides Archie's father John, his three oldest siblings were threadmill workers in 1891.

The construction of Coats Sao Paulo factory began in 1907. The factory was located at Iparanga, a district of Sao Paulo, where the Brazilian operation of Coats called Coats Linhas Corcente was based.

No doubt, news of the new factory in Brazil would be discussed by the workforce at Coats Anchor Mill in Paisley. One wonders if Archie McLean would have been aware of these discussions, or even thought that in a few years he would be living and working in Sao Paulo.

The headquarters of the Coats group and its principle mills in Brazil, are located in the district of Ipiranga in Sao Paulo. With the growth of population and demand for their product, Coats built a new mill in Sao Paulo in 1953. This mill is located at Vila Ema, 5 minutes from Ipiranga and is one of the most modern thread mills in the world.

As time went on, import restrictions were imposed, and difficulties with exchange rates were experienced more and more. Production was transferred to Brazil to produce articles from their own cotton stocks.

The thread mills in Sao Paulo were supplied with spoolwood and empty spools from the forestland sawmills and turnings plant from the facility which the company owned in Southern Brazil.

Cotton is grown in Brazil, and is referred to as perennial cotton. The trees will grow to four feet and yield a crop for 10 years or so. In the south of Brazil shorter cotton called Paulista is grown. This allows the Brazilian operation to be self sufficient.

This was the operation which Archie McLean and his colleagues from Paisley were sent to Sao Paulo to build, and to train the locals to run.

Archie McLean's first known team was a Barrhead team, then called Arthurlie, followed by Bute Athletic, and then Perthshire in the Glasgow Junior league. In Scotland there are still thriving 'Junior Football Leagues'. Junior in this case relates to the level of standard of play, rather than the age of the players. Junior football at the time Archie played, was a source Senior clubs in Scotland and England, used to find new talent.

While playing Junior football Archie played in a trial representative match between Ayrshire and Renfrewshire, but missed out on playing for the Scottish team at Junior level.

Senior teams were continually having scouts attend the Glasgow Junior leagues to find new talent. Arsenal probably became aware of McLean through a scout, and during their Scottish visit in 1908 they made contact with him. This was in the spring of 1908. Arsenal at this time were known as 'Woolwich Arsenal' and during their brief Scottish tour, they invited Archie to join up with the team. He made two appearances, but no offer was made for Archie to become an Arsenal player. Arsenal then, as they are at the start of the twenty first century, were a leading English team, joining them would have been a great opportunity for Archie.

There must have been disappointment that Arsenal didn't offer McLean a contract, but he didn't have to wait long to have the chance to play senior football, as opposed to the junior football he had been playing with Perthshire.

On a summer evening of 1908, there was a knock on

the door of Archie McLean's home in Paisley. Archie had already gone to bed. He was awakened, and told that a director of Ayr FC wanted to talk to him. Archie went to the door of his home, and then and there he signed on. This was how Archie McLean was to enter senior football in Scotland. Archie was signed to replace a player who had moved to England.

Senior football offered Archie a better deal. He would receive more money, he would be playing with and against better players, and there would be much more press coverage of the games he played in. Archie by 1910 had a day job at Coats' Mill in Paisley where he was a machine mechanic.

Archie was to spend 2 seasons with Ayr, who played the second division of the Scottish League. The correspondent on the 'Ayr Observer' reported on the Scottish cup tie against Hibernian at Easter Road, the Edinburgh home of Hibs. The game was played on January 1909, and Archie played on the right wing. The report stated that Archie had a brilliant run down the wing, but the ball was ballooned high over the cross bar. Archie's performance on the right wing for Ayr varied. In some games everything went right for Archie but other days were not his. Mercurial is a word that comes to mind to describe Archie's game in the Ayr days.

The formation for teams in 1909 was the traditional 2-3-5 with two full backs, 3 in midfield, a right half, centre wall and left half, and the 5 playing 'up front', with an inside right, centre forward and inside left, and two players who were referred to as wingers, a right winger and a left winger.

Later developments in the formation as teams, led to
4-4-2 and several variations, where teams play with two
'wing backs, ' who have defensive and attractive roles,
unlike Archie, whose role was to focus on attack. In the
Euro 2004 semi final between Portugal and Holland in June
2004, Cristiano Ronaldo was seen defending in his own
penalty area one minute, and the next racing down the
wing and making a cross into the Holland penalty area. As
footnote to those comments, Ronaldo scored with a header
in a game Portugal won 2-1.

The Ayr club amalgamated with another Ayr team
Parkhouse in 1910, to become Ayr United, and played at
Somerset Park, as the club still in existence in the
beginning of the twenty first century.

The Ayr Observer reported that the directors of the
newly formed Ayr United were unable to come to an
agreement with Archie McLean, as he seemed to want
better terms than the new Ayr United were prepared to
meet.

Archie signed for the Scottish Union League team
Galston, in Ayrshire near Kilmarnock. It is difficult to
understand why Archie made this change, in that Galston
was not easy to get to from Paisley, Ayr, on the other hand,
was on a main rail route. The standard of the football, and
the money paid, would have been a drop from what Ayr
United had to offer, but other factors may have influenced
the decision to move club. Archie's brief spell at Galston
was successful, and he was on the score sheet in his first
three games for his new club.

Galston played Ayr United Archie's former club in the Ayrshire League, and he would have been pleased with the 3-0 win. Later in the season, Galston were drawn against Celtic in the Scottish Cup. The away tie resulted in a 0-1 defeat. Galston played in the Scottish Union League, and this result against the mighty Celtic at Parkhead in Glasgow, was a result which left the Ayrshire club with pride in their narrow defeat.

Archie seemed to have a 'Wander Lust', in that his time at Galston was short lived. He moved to Abercorn, a team that in 1911 played in Union League and had their ground in Paisley.

A report in September of that year indicated that Archie was now playing for Johnstone, a town a few miles west of Paisley, and by December a report in the Paisley and Renfrewshire gazette ran a headline 'McLean cleverly scores winning goal'.

This was in a game against Peebles Rovers, when Johnstone won 3-2. Johnstone played their games at Newfield which was near where the Johnstone West railway station was located.

On 13th December 1909, Archie married Margaret McNeil. At that time Archie was twenty three years old and employed in Anchor Mill as a threadmill tender. He was living at 54 Causeyside Street in Paisley and Margaret worked at the same mill presumably. She was twenty one and her home was at 6 Clarence Street in the town. The records indicate that the marriage took place at this address and was conducted by the Church of Scotland. Archie and Margaret moved to 18 Alice Street in Paisley on 22

October 1910. Archie and Margaret were blessed with two sons Jack and Robert, and were able to celebrate fifty years of marriage. At this time of their marriage, Margaret who was also known as 'Bel' or 'Bessy', would surely have expected to live out her life in the shadow of the mill complex at Anchor. She had no idea that in a few short years she would be living on the other side of the world in a land where the people spoke Portuguese, and the culture was so different to the Paisley of the early twentieth century and to Scotland.

Duncan Carmichael a historian on the "History of Football in Ayr", has written books on aspects of this subject. One of the books that Duncan wrote was entitled ' Ayr United Football Club' Vol 1 - 1886 - 1939. No reference appears to Archie in any of Duncan's publications.

To a measure, the balance was redressed in the Ayr United match day programme for their match against Stranraer in the Scottish Football League division one, on Saturday 2nd January 1999.

The following notes on Archie were included in this programme, when it was stated that it was unusual that a player who graced the Ayr FC team at Somerset Park went on to make international appearances for Brazil, against Chile and Argentina. The article went on to say that Archie's football career in Brazil was well documented, but little is known about his involvement in football in Scotland .

For the 1911-12 season Archie played for Johnstone Football Club. At that time Johnstone was a member of the

Scottish Union League. That season was a successful one. The club won the Victoria Cup, which was a local competition, when they defeated Arthurlie from Barrhead after a replay.

For a small club like Johnstone, the Scottish Cup provided finance with a successful run. That season unfortunately they were knocked out of the Scottish Cup at the qualifying cup stage of the competition, and participated in the Consolation Cup which was run by the Scottish Football Association. The Consolation Cup gave the clubs involved the consolation of having the opportunity for success, and also to gain much needed finance with a successful cup run, after having been knocked out of the main cup competition.

The final was played at Rugby Park, the home of Kilmarnock Football Club, with a crowd of some three thousand spectators present. Despite having the bright sun in their eyes in the first half, Johnstone were two nil up, at half time.

Archie scored the first goal, and Johnstone ran out four-nil winners against Galston. This was the last season Johnstone played in the Scottish Union. The following season Johnstone were successful in their application to join the second division of the Scottish League, but were without Archie McLean.

At the end of what turned out to be his last season in Scottish football and with the Johnstone Club, Archie and two other players took part in a social gathering, which although he didn't realise it at the time, was a farewell to the Johnstone Football Club. Archie was a participant in an evening of reading and songs. This was a good memory to take with him for his future life in Brazil, and the end of his football career in Scotland.

By 1910, Archie was working for J and P Coats at their Anchor Mill in Paisley. His job there was as a technician, a machine mechanic. The job was referred to as a tenter in the finishing department, and he combined working and playing football. He may have hoped that a move would come in his life as result of his football skills, but it was his abilities as a tenter that gave him the opportunity to move from Paisley.

By 1912, Archie was playing successfully for Johnstone. He was looking forward to the start of a new season, having played a significant part in the Johnstone triumph, in the Consolation Cup final, with a win over his former club Galston.

Coats asked Archie to go to Brazil to the company's large mill at Ipiranga, Sao Paulo, which operated under the name of Campanhia Brasiliera De Linhas Para Coser. Archie had a contract for three months, and in that his football team Johnstone expected, and hoped he would return, they took out a registration for him, for the 1912-13 season. Not only did Archie fail to return, after his initial contract was completed, but he was to stay on in Sao Paulo for the best part of forty years.

Consolacao was the district of Sao Paulo in which Archie was to live, work, and play for the next 37 years of his life, and the contrast to Paisley was very marked.

Five

<u>O VEADINHO(The Little Deer)</u>

Archie was in Paisley until June 1912. He then travelled to Southampton, to board the Royal Mail's ship The Aragon on 7th June 1912 to sail to Santos, as Charles Miller has done in 1894. A local newspaper, The Paisley and Renfrewshire Gazette, on 21st June 1912 reported that Archie had been called to Brazil on business, with the inference that his visit to Brazil would be brief.

Shortly after arriving in Sao Paulo, Archie sent a post card to Robert Steel, who was the Works Manager at the Anchor thread Mill in Paisley. In the brief note to Mr. Steel, Archie indicated he liked Brazil, but found that the prices in Brazil were much higher than in Scotland. He indicated, that time was 'wearing on' and that he had assumed he would be in Sao Paulo, only for a few months .

He was looking forward to being back in Paisley again soon, and one wonders how he would have felt, if he had known at that time that he was to spend nearly forty years in Sao Paulo.

On his arrival in Sao Paulo, apart from settling into his role in the factory, Archie was no doubt anxious to find out what was the possibility of playing football, and what the standard would be. Archie would have appreciated all that Charles Miller and others had done to establish football in the Sao Paulo area, and that a British team (SPAC), Sao Paulo Athletics Club was part of a local league, the Liga

Paulista. He would also have been delighted to discover that at the factory, there were a number of Scots, managers and technicians, who had played football in the Paisley area, and wanted to take up the game in their new home town.

Archie had two teams he would play for, SPAC and a new team called 'The Scottish Wanderers'. They played in royal blue strips and white shorts, and the lion rampant badge adorned their shirts. These men may have not wanted to be in Brazil, and were indeed wanderers from Scotland who would have felt less home sick with the possibility of playing football in Sao Paulo.

As early as August 1912, there was mention in the press in Sao Paulo of a team which was referred to as the 'Scottish Wanderers'. On 11 August 1912, a team from the British workforce at the J& P Coats Sao Paulo thread mill was formed. The team played a 2-3-5 formation, with Archie McLean playing at centre forward against SC International's Extra team. Archie was involved in getting the Wanderers off the ground and the team played friendly games, as the players were glad to continue their involvement with football in Sao Paulo. On September 1st 1912, Archie played his first game for SPAC in the Liga Paulista. The game was against CA Ipiranga, a team from the district of Sao Paulo where Coats factory was located. SPAC won the game 7-0, and there is no record of Archie scoring in this game. The local paper O Estado de Sao Paulo reported that McLean had a positive influence on the win, and had made his presence felt on Paulista Football.

Later in September 1912, a team called the Argentinos

were in Sao Paulo, and an eleven was selected to oppose them. It's not clear if Archie was selected for the eleven who lost the game 6-3. One player who did play in the team on the left wing, was Arthur Friedenreith who was an aspiring young Brazilian, of whom more will be said later. O Estado would report on the Wanderers matches, but gave no mention of the score. The reporter did like Archie's contribution on the wing. He stated that McLean was very clever on the ball, and his play greatly pleased the Brazilians.

For the 1913 season, SPAC was no longer in the Liga, and Archie was invited to join SC Americano, who were the 1912 champions. The season proved successful for both McLean and his new team who retained their league championship.

A new league was established by Associacao Paulista De Esportes Athleticos (APEL), whose directors had the objective to maintain what they talked of as 'social distinctions' in sport. These directors persuaded the Scottish Wanderers to join this new league for season 1914, as they felt that having accomplished British Footballers in the league, would help to establish it.

There was a resumption of matches between Rio and Sao Paulo. In November 1913, the two districts met at Fluminenses ground, when the teams competed for a cup donated by a newspaper in Rio. The Sao Paulo team representing Liga Paulista had only one player from Britain, namely the Scot Archie McLean from Paisley.

When Archie arrived in Brazil, they were beginning to develop a style of football, which was becoming uniquely

Brazilian. McLean was able to have British involvement in this development in the Sao Paulo area, and despite the fact that the Sao Paulo Athletic Club no longer participated in the local Liga, Archie was good enough to play for other teams. Not only did he hold down this place, but he had a distinct influence on how the game developed in the Sao Paulo area.

Archie developed a special partnership with an Englishman Bill Hopkins, both for the Sao Paulo district team and for the Scottish Wanderers. Bill Hopkins was born in 1889 in thePortsmouth/Southampton area ,and he was employed for Standard Oil in the Sao Paulo area. He never married, and lived the rest of his life in Brazil after moving from England, and in fact died in Sao Paulo.

When the season began in April 1914, Archie was the only player who had played in the 1912 season for the Wanderers. The partnership between Archie and Bill was to be extremely successful, as they played short interpassing on the run. This style of play was called 'Tabelinha' by the Brazilian. It means' The Little Chart'.

Archie was very versatile in the positions he could play, but his best position was as a forward, either playing at outside left or as an inside left. In fact Bill and Archie were introducing to the Brazilians what is now referred to as old fashioned wing play. This involved passing and interpassing between the player who played as the winger and the inside forward. The Brazilians gave Archie the nickname of O Veadinho, which translated means 'the little deer'. These locals could appreciate his great turn of pace and agility.

The 1914 season was a disaster for the Scottish Wanderers, with accusations of rough play and violent conduct. For the season 1915, they had changed their name to the Wanderers, and they continued to play this season in the APEL league. At the end of the 1915 season there was a move to throw the Wanderers out of the Liga Paulista. This was based on the feeling that the Wanderers were professional, as they divided the gate money between the players. The behaviour of the team the previous season did not help them, as well as concerns over how the club was being run. The governing body of the Liga brought a club called Palestra Italia into the Liga to gain the support of the growing Italian Community in Sao Paulo.

In the 1916 season, both Archie McLean and the now 41 year old Charles Miller were included in the pool of referees. McLean and Hopkins moved to play for Athletico Sao Bento in the 1916 season, and helped their new team to finish second in the Liga. A press report in June 1916 extolled the virtue of the play of Archie and Bill .
The directors of the APEL were concerned to 'maintain standards' to allow football to be the preserve of the elite. But the times were changing, football was growing in popularity and becoming the people's game.
As the differences developed in Sao Paulo football circles and beyond, Charles Miller still had an association with the Liga Paulista by being on the referees' list. However, Archie McLean, who came from a background in Paisley where football was a passport beyond working class roots, was involved with the elite APEL league, whose directors

wanted to maintain the status and have football as an activity for those and such as those in Sao Paulo.

Archie was recognised and chosen for various representative teams in 1914. He and Bill Hopkins played for a Paulista eleven against Cariocas. McLean played an influential role in the win and the draw against this select from the Rio league. Archie never played for the Brazilian National Team, but he did however play for SC Americano against a foreign side, which was referred to as an International match.

By 1916, Archie was playing for a team called Sao Bento, and teamed up with Bill Hopkins for what was a successful season in the league. Like Charles Miller, Archie refereed, and in the 1916 season he was listed on the referee's panel.

Archie continued to turn out for Sao Bento in seasons 1917, 1918 and 1919. In January 1920 he was part of their team for a tournament organised by A. A. das Palmeiras.

Archie was a talented dribbler and skilled passer of the ball. In his play he scrapped the traditional long ball to concentrate on developing skills, and he introduced a short passing game that was played in a more fluid way. This style of play was suited to Archie's abilities of being nimble and fleet of foot as he played on the wing.

The effect of this change of approach, from the way Charles Miller had learned his football in Southampton, was latched onto by clubs and players in Sao Paulo. Archie was instrumental in helping make this change happen, and this was the way other areas of Brazil such as Rio began to develop their play.

The Sao Paulo story is as old as Brazil is. Two Jesuits established a mission on a high plateau 70km(42 miles) from the coast in 1554, and they called the colony Sao Paulo. Sao Paulo was isolated, and located far from the centre of things such as administration and commercial activities. In the early days of the life of Sao Paulo, few European women came to live there, as life was hard and there were few comforts. The male colonists who were mainly from Portuguese origins, would father children to Amerindian women. These mixed race offspring were hardy, and grew up being asked to deal with the hardships of frontier life.

By the nineteenth century, the Paulista (as the residents of Sao Paulo state are called) had a major influence in two significant events in Brazilian history, namely the fight against slavery and the establishment of a Republic in 1889. In the early nineteenth century, the Paulista plantation owners grew cotton as they became aware of the growth of the textile industry in Britain, but then moved into coffee where competition wasn't as fierce, and where the fertile soil was ideally suited for the coffee bush to grow.

Between 1870 and 1920 more than 2 million immigrants worker settled in the Sao Paulo areas to work mainly on the coffee plantations.

The growth in Sao Paulo population has been staggering:

1872	32,000
1890	65,000
1920	579,000
1960	3,800,000

2002   18,000,000

(Compared with the 11million population of Rio de Janeiro in 2002)

At the beginning of twenty-first century, Sao Paulo is the worlds third largest city. In fact Sao Paulo was a tenth of the Brazilian population in the 1960's,(only New York and Tokyo had larger populations) . In the 1970's, Sao Paulo was the world's fastest growing city, with 1000 new residents arriving each day.

One wonders what Charles Miller and Archie McLean would think of the Sao Paulo in the twenty first century and its ever growing population.

Archie would have loved the development of football in the city and in Brazil. He would have felt he had been born 100 years too early. Archie, with his football skills, could have played in the Scottish or English premier leagues – Charles, on the other hand, would have had no truck with anything involving professionalism in sport. The culture that allowed for cricket matches to be played in England between the Gentleman (the amateurs) and the Players (the professionals who could not afford to play for the fun of it), could not be maintained in the twentieth century, as football became a global sport.
This was what Charles was about, being a gentleman, and he was fortunate to be able to maintain those attitudes and enjoy the lifestyle he did.

Despite the differences in lots of aspects of their background, attitudes and lifestyles, the two men had one thing in common, they both loved sports. It seemed all sports which were played with a ball anyway. Football, tennis and golf were particular favourites and Archie could add billiards and bowls to the list of sports in which he took part.

Both men had loved the Sao Paulo Athletic Club and used the facilities extensively. The club is still at the same location as it has been since the 1890's, and they both would have been shocked and disappointed at the developments which have taken place in the twenty-first century.

The Club is very exclusive today, and is guarded by tall gates and staff who check all those who wish to enter the club. Tennis, bowls and swimming are played by those whose language is Portuguese not English. It is interesting that the turf for the bowling green was originally brought all the way from Scotland, and is probably the best grass surface in this part of Brazil. Nowadays, the majority of the members are Brazilians who are wealthy. Those Brazilians enjoy the sports facilities of the athletics club, but are attracted by the English background of the club and the ambience of the club house. On the menu for one evening is Chicken Curry. No doubt Charles Miller would have had Steak and Kidney pudding as the English alternative.

Six
<u>Haggis Row</u>

Archie and Margaret came to love life in Sao Paulo.
Archie loved the vibrant Latin American culture and the
Brazilian language, which he spoke fluently. The family
home was at 62 Rua Jorgi Morreira in Sao Paulo, which
because of the number of Scottish families who were
associated with the Coats' factory, was affectionately
called Haggis Row. The Coats' employees lived on this
street, where the homes were well appointed, and the envy
of the employees of other British companies who lived in
Sao Paulo. There was a row of 11 houses, which was a ten
minute tram ride from the Brazilian factory for sewing
threads.

In "Brazilian", the company was known as Compania
Brasileira of Linara Para Coser (CBLC). The factory was
located in the Ipiranga District of Sao Paulo. The other
Scottish families knew Archie as 'Uncle Mac'. All the
manufacturing from the beginning to the 'finishing' was
carried out at the Ipiranga Mill. Some of the staff who
were assigned to Sao Paulo had previously had contact
with Coats' operations in Portugal, and found variations in
Portuguese spoken in Brazil compared with that spoken in
Portugal.

Moving from Paisley to Sao Paulo brought to Archie
and Margaret McLean many different experiences. For
Archie, familiar activities, such as working in the factory
and playing football, were important parts of his life . A
sight which was familiar from their time in Paisley, was the

tram. Sao Paulo as Paisley had a tram system.

In Paisley , the Paisley District Tram Company
existed from 1903 till 1923. Prior to this time, William
Murphy who came from Dublin, stole a march on the Town
Council of Paisley, by running trams. The Murphy's trams
were known as 'The Murphies' by the locals. In an age
when working families did not own a car, the trams were
referred to as the 'poor man's motor car'. These electric
tram cars replaced the horse drawn trams, and were
operated by Paisley's own Tramway Company. The
tramcars were open on the upper deck, despite the
inclement weather for much of the year. The Tram system
came from Glasgow, through Paisley Cross, and then out
to a depot in Elderslie , west of Paisley. The system also
went to Hawkhead Road, and to the Potterhill area in the
south end of the town.

From the history of the Ipiranga Mill by J.S. Nesbitt,
outlined in Chapter eleven, the house Archie and Margaret
McLean moved into, in the Rue Jorge Morreira was not
built until the 1920s. The McLeans would have been
thrilled with this home, and particularly the 'modern'
bathroom. Back in Alice Street in Paisley , they had an
'outside' toilet on the tenement stairway . The Macleans'
home in Paisley had no bath, and to have a bath, they
would have gone to the public baths, part of the swimming
baths complex in Storie Street, near to the town centre and
located opposite the local cattle market. In some areas of
Paisley , it would the 1970s before all old tenement
properties had bathrooms installed.

In 1939, Archie was the head tenter (a machine

mechanic) in the finishing department with the two other Scots Hector McNeil and Eddie Harrison. The head of the department was Scottish, and there were 2000 employees in the finishing department. A machine mechanic would maintain the spooling machines.

Archie had been able to learn Portuguese, which in Archie's case, would have been described as 'working Portuguese'. The work force at the Ipiranga mill was cosmopolitan. Besides the Scots there were Brazilian, Germans and Italians in the factory. Archie and the other British managers, engineers and technicians had a role to train and instruct the local workforce, and to be able to speak to them in their native tongue was a significant part of their responsibility. Archie had no special status at work because of his football exploits. He was one of the workforce, and that only.

There was a lot of social contact between the Scottish families. They would visit each other on a regular basis, dropping into each others' homes as they would have done back home in Scotland, with no formal invitation necessary.

They enjoyed a colonial lifestyle, St Andrew's nights and related social activities were part of their lives. There was even a St Andrew's Ladies Society formed for the wives of the Scots in Sao Paulo. These Scots worked almost exclusively for Coats, apart from a few Scots, who worked for a factory called The Juta Flax company, which had its Scottish operation in Dundee, and did work for the Sao Paulo railway company.

It seemed if you were Scots you were someone. The

St Andrews Society was run by Scots, however members of the English community who were also far from home, were invited to participate in Scottish social events. Eileen Wallis, who is the guardian of the archives and history of the St. Andrews's Society in Sao Paulo, has provided the following information about Archie's involvement in the St Andrew's Society.

Archibald F McLean – one of the founding members of the St Andrew's Society of the State of Sao Paulo. Born in Paisley, Archie McLean came to Brazil for Linhas (now Coats Corrente) in 1912. Expecting to stay for a period of months, he finally returned to Scotland on his retirement in 1949.

Archie was the Society's eighteenth President in 1941 and he remained in office because of the second World War, until1949 . In addition to being a Founding Member, he served as a Committee member in 1928 and 1931, and was Vice-President of the Society in 1939 and 1940. To Archie, fell the honour of chairing the first post-second World War Banquet in 1945, while on 16th March, 1949 he also presided at the meeting held to re-start the Society. A keen Freemason, he was Past Master of the Centenary Lodge. His two sons were members of the Society and, indeed, Robert the younger, became not only the first Brazilian born President of our Society, but also the first son of a past President to be elected to this office.

Archie McLean had a vast circle of friends and acquaintances. Perhaps he can best be described in a phrase contained in a letter about Archie received from one of our overseas correspondents, when he referred to Archie

"As a most loveable Scot".

Apart from one of the Scottish managers who was a bachelor, Archie was the only Scots employee of Coats with a car. He drove a 'Chevie' (a chevrolet). As work at the factory stopped at lunch time on Saturdays, he and his wife Margaret would drive off in the afternoon. Margaret was referred to as 'The Duchess' by the other Scots families, as she dressed very stylishly . They would go to the SPAC, where Archie could indulge in his love of sport by playing tennis or bowls when his days of playing football were over. Instead of going to SPAC ,they would have driven to the country club, where Archie could play another of his favourite sports namely golf.

Archie was keen to continue his association with football, a game he really loved, by attending football, and he was recognised at the games he attended and knew the officials. Despite his love for football, Archie was contracted to Coats, and the company came first. Before Archie left for Sao Paulo, he might have joined a team and played for a living in Scotland or more likely England. But in those days, the money wasn't good playing football on a full time basis, and for a working married man in the West of Scotland Coats' offered security that football didn't . A secure job with long term future prospects was important.

From a football point of view, Archie's legacy was the scientific way he and others, particularly Bill Hopkins played, the tactics they used and the ability to employ their physical assets such as being nimble and playing with pace. Archie and Bill Hopkins developed an intricate passing movement, which was a feature of their play, and much admired by locals who enjoyed watching them play. Although Archie was an amateur, he did enjoy various gifts in appreciation of his skill and flair. On one occasion, Archie was persuaded off the golf course to play in a game, and found £80 in his car after the game, in appreciation of his play. After another game Archie, when changed to go home, found in his jacket pocket vouchers to allow him to go and be measured for two new suits, in the days when suits were all made to measure. Archie and his family enjoyed a good standard of living in Brazil, maybe quite a bit better than they might have done, had Archie and Margaret stayed in Paisley.

There were two major events in the Annual Social Calendar of the St Andrew's Society of Sao Paulo. One was the St Andrews day celebrations on the last Thursday in November. St.Andrew is the patron saint of Scotland. The other was on January 25[th,] the Annual Burns Supper to commemorate the life of Robert Burns, Scotland's National Poet. The Burns Supper included the traditional menu of "tatties, neeps and haggis".

Coats Anchor Mills in Paisley had a progressive outlook in catering for its staff and this included sports, recreational and social activities. However, they would not have been on the scale they were to experience in Sao Paulo as part of the British community in the first half of the twentieth century.

Archie was sent to Brazil, initially on a short term contract. He boarded the Royal Mail's Aragon at Southampton on 7 June 1912 to sail to Santos.

The journey to Santos in Brazil by ship took more than two weeks and then a train ride of the 39 miles to Sao Paulo, with the Sao Paulo Railway Company. The ships would call in at Rio De Janeiro. Travel from Scotland was with the London Midland and Scottish Railway Company to Tilbury the port for London, and then by Royal Mail or Blue Star ship to Brazil.

Coats allowed their managers far more luxurious travel taking a boat from Southampton. Archie's status as a technician did not allow him to use the route from Southampton. By the 1940,s travel by ship was with the Highland line, and one of their ships on this route was the Highland Chieftain.

Archie could be described as dapper with his distinctive 'bow' tie. Long after his football days were over, he still kept fit and active and enjoyed sport.

On return to Scotland, Archie and Margaret set up home in Auchmannoch Avenue in the Ralston area of Paisley. Ralston is in the East end of Paisley next to the Glasgow boundary, 'a most sought after part of the town to live in'. They must have appreciated the contrast with 13 Alice Street, their home in 1912.

Archie does not seem to have been an extrovert, so the participation in the celebration of the Consolation Cup win seemed almost out of character to his usual quiet and unassuming personality. Back in Paisley, Archie and Margaret could enjoy their 'blethers' in the High Street as they stopped and spoke with friends and acquaintances.

His golfing would now be at Elderslie Golf course, 5 miles from Archie's new home. Grass bowling would now be at the Anchor Bowling Club, which was part of the facilities that Coats Mills provided for their employees. The bowling green consisted of 2 greens and a lovely little club house, which were located in a beautiful peaceful setting in the shadow of the Mile End Building, (at the East End of the Anchor mill complex). The bowling club was founded in 1896 and the original 'Bowl House' is now a listed building. The club built a new clubhouse, which was a wooden structured building opposite to the 'Bowl House'. This would have been familiar to Archie. When not participating in competitions, Archie would have taken part in scratch session which were called 'Wappenschaws'. Members at the bowling club still remember Archie and refer to him as a "gentleman".

Archie was able to enjoy spectator football at St Mirren Love Street ground, rather than Pacaembu Stadium in Sao Paulo. The Scottish game in the years Archie watched, was a fast and furious contest, with players having little or no time on the ball before a tackle came.

In 1965, the St. Mirren manager was Doug Milward. A Brazilian agent, Senor Ramas persuaded St. Mirren to take Fernando Azeveoo, a centre forward. Doug Milward was assured Azeveoo would score lots of goals. He was given a game against local rivals Greenock Morton, on September 11th 1965. Morton won the game 1 - 0, and Fernando was not a success, so never played again for St. Mirren .

No doubt Archie McLean, who regularly attended the St. Mirren home games, would have been called upon during the negotiations, to act as a translator for the

Brazilians. Senor Ramas seemed to be a very persuasive person, and Celtic and Dunfermline gave Fernando, and another Brazilian a trial, but neither team was impressed. Archie, may have been called upon by Celtic and Dunfermline to act as interpreter. Brazilian players have not made any great impact in Scotland, where the weather and the style of football is very different, from that in Brazil.

The Love Street ground consisted of a small stand where the spectator, by paying a higher entrance fee, could sit to enjoy the game. The rest of the ground consisted of open terracing, where the fans had to stand with no protection from the variances of the Scottish winter.

Archie kept the extrovert side of his nature for the football pitch, where he was a different personality with a ball at his feet, and a crowd roaring their anticipation and approval. In other aspects of his life he was shy and quiet. The contrast between living in a tenement in Alice Street in the South side of Paisley, and having as your home a villa in Sao Paulo was such, that the McLeans must have reflected from time to time on this contrast. No longer could they walk down Paisley High Street and meet people they knew and stop for a 'blether'. They would have missed this social interaction.

As families returned from Brazil having retired, done their tour of duty, or wanted to be around their children as they provided them with a Scottish education, they developed what might be referred to as the Paisley Sao Paulo Group. They knew each other from Sao Paulo, and made every effort to stay in touch with each other as they returned mainly to the West of Scotland. Even in the 21st century, this network still exists, although with the passage of time, the group has become smaller, but it is still close knit. Archie and Margaret were very much a part of this group, and enjoyed their involvement with their Sao Paulo friends back in Paisley.

Seven

Then and Now and the Beautiful Team

Sao Paulo's Campeonata de Futebol was the first organised tournament in Brazil, and started in 1901.
The first Club Associacao Athletica of Mackenzie College, in Sao Paulo, was in fact founded in 1898. The Confebracao Brazilfira de desportos (CBD) was founded in 1914, and joined FIFA in 1923.
As the development of football took hold in Brazil, in 1950 a Rio-Sao Paulo tournament was established. Brazil hosted the World Cup, and was beaten 2-1 in the final by Uruguay.

By 1935 a professional league was established in Sao Paulo, and the decades that followed were a peak for the city, with a rash of stadium building and the arrival of Pele at Santos. In the twenty first century in Sao Paulo there are the following teams: Corinthians, who were formed in 1910 by railway workers, and were named after the English amateurs who had recently toured the city. They played in black and white. Santos was founded in 1912 and was Pele's team. Palmeiras was founded in 1914 and play in green and white. The club was founded by Italian immigrants. Sao Paulo was founded in 1935, and compared with the other teams in Sao Paulo, has a magnificent ground with a capacity of 80,000. Each of the Sao Paulo teams has won the national championships on several occasions with the Palmeiras club being the most successful to date since the national leagues inception in

1971. It is a reflection of the standard of football played by these four teams, that each has won the World Club Cup. Beside a national league, the cup competition is called the Copa de Brazil. These are state leagues which run at the early part of the season which means that football in Brazil is played all the year round.

In 1902, the Sao Paulo championship was won by the Sao Paulo Athletics Club, who won the championship for the first three years of it's existence, and for the four of the first ten years. In the years 2001 and 2003, Corinthians were winners of the league which they had first won back in 1922, and they are still the dominant force in all the competitions they take part in.

It is interesting to reflect on how Charles Miller and Archie McLean would have felt about football in Sao Paulo and in Brazil, and the country's dominance in the World Cup in the second half of the twentieth century.

After the Brazilians' failure in England in the 1966 World Cup Finals, in preparation for the 1970 finals in Mexico, one and a half million dollars was spent to ensure that the team would have every opportunity to do well. Pele was persuaded to return for these finals, after the rough treatment he had received in England by the European teams. The dictatorship in Brazil was anxious for victory, and to exploit any success. The final was against Italy, each had two victories, so whoever won would keep the Jules Rimet trophy for good. There were 107,000 in the stadium, and an estimated 8000 million watching on TV.

During the final, Brazil had scored their one

hundredth World Cup goal, and their fourth goal in the final, scored by Carlos Alberto, was acknowledged as a great goal. The score was 4-1 for Brazil, who were able to keep the trophy. Back in Brazil, there was great rejoicing, with the nation experiencing a feeling of community and brotherhood, and that all the expense had been worthwhile.

It is acknowledged that the 1970 World Cup won by Brazil, had been achieved by the best team the world had seen. The team included Pele, Rivellino, Garrincho, Gerson and Carlos Alberto, and has been described as the 'Beautiful Team'. Reflecting on the factors which produced such a special team, the following were considered fundamental ingredients:

- The climate of Brazil
- The ethnic mix that makes the country what it is
- The poverty of the country
- The peerless passion for futebol, above all other sport, all over Brazil

Carlos Alberto who scored in that memorable World Cup Final, was of the opinion that Brazilians are not tall or strong, but are suited to football. That's just the way they are. Archie McLean fitted that bill as he wasn't particularly tall or strong, but he was indeed suited to football.

The Journal de Brazil in June 1970 compared Brazil's victory in the World Cup finals with the ball, to the conquest of the moon by the Americans. The journalist and writer Hugh McIlvaney commented, that the Brazilian team of 1970 may have represented the highest point of beauty and sophistication the game is destined to reach.

Pier Paulo Pasolini made a comparison of the European and South American approach to playing football. Pier talks about European teams being prose, tough, premeditated, systematic and collective, whereas South American teams are poetry, ductile, spontaneous, individual and exotic. Could this reflect on the way Charles Miller, played compared with Archie McLean's approach to playing the game?

During the 1970 World Cup, ITV had as part of its panel, Malcolm Allison and Paddy Crerand. At one point in a discussion on the Brazilian team and Pele in particular, Allison asked the question 'How do you spell Pele'? In reply, the quick witted Crerand replied, 'Easy, G-O-D' which was a measure of Pele's influence on the 1970 Brazilian team.

The World Cup was called the Jules Rimet Trophy, and was the first global tournament for professional teams who competed on a national basis. The first competition was held in Uruguay, in 1930, none of the British teams took part. This World Cup competition was initiated by Jules Rimet, who was the FIFA President. FIFA was founded in 1907. In 1958, Scotland, England, Ireland and Wales all qualified to take part in the finals. In the beginning 16 teams took part, but this was later increased to 32 teams, mainly for commercial reasons. Prior to 1930, the only World Football tournament was strictly for amateur players, at the Olympic Games.

During the 2002 final between Brazil and Germany, at one point in the game the TV camera focused on the crowd, rather than the game. The camera zoomed in on a banner

which had the following written in English in large letters and hand printed. The banner said 'God is Brazilian'.
It is the case that those who live in Rio de Janeiro and Sao Paulo, indeed feel that 'God is Brazilian', that they have the best country in the world, and the best football team to match their great country.
Brazil's national stadium is the Maracana Stadium in Rio De Janeiro. It was built for the 1950 World Cup finals. The final of the tournament was between Brazil and Uruguay, and attracted a crowd of almost 200,000. Due to safety regulations, it is unlikely that this record will ever be broken. Among the innovations was the world's largest cantilevered roof, and the stadium also contained lifts. Sadly, the stadium is now in a poor state of repair, and unsafe. Crowds of only 10,000 are now commonplace.

Scotland qualified for the World Cup Finals in West Germany in 1974. They were drawn in group two for the first round with Brazil, Yugoslavia and Zaire. Sixteen teams had qualified for the finals, and round one would reduce the teams to eight. From there the two teams at the top of the two mini leagues qualified for the final. Scotland played Brazil at Frankfurt on June 18th 1974, and came away with a nil-nil draw, having previously drawn nil-nil, with Yugoslavia and beat Zaire two-nil. Sadly, although they finished on the same points total as Brazil and Yugoslavia, Scotland lost out on goal difference, and finished in third place in group two, and were eliminated.

The game against Brazil saw Scotland perform at a level, not previously seen by a Scottish team that was the better team on the day. Brazil's silky skills deserted them, and they were reduced to fouling the Scottish players to stop their progress towards the Brazilian goal. Billy Bremner of Leeds United was dynamic, and chased and harried and did all he could to win the points for Scotland, but to no avail.

Scotland's manager was Willie Ormond. He had played for Hibernian the Edinburgh team who had a famous forward line, and Willie was one of their stars. He came from Musselbrough, near Edinburgh and was a loveable man who told the journalists about his team stating, 'The lads had done well'.

Scotland had not got past the first round but did come home from West Germany the only unbeaten team. The final winners West Germany, had lost one-nil to their neighbours East Germany in the first round. By the time the 1974 World Cup game between Brazil and Scotland was played, Archie McLean had died. Had he still been alive, the press would have no doubt interviewed him, as they did at the time of the Brazilian World Cup victory in Mexico in 1970 with their 'Dream Team'.

The Brazilian team of 1974 was not the force it was in 1970, as they were an ageing team, and vulnerable in ways that they were not in their triumph in Mexico. The Scots had availed themselves well, and such were their resources, Celtic's Jimmy Johnstone didn't feature in any of their games in Germany.

The forwards who did play in the 1974 finals were:
- Kenny Dalglish
- Peter Lorimer

- Joe Jordan
- Denis Law
- Willie Morgan

Dalglish was playing for Celtic in 1974, and Law, Lorimer and Morgan played in England in 1974. During his career, Joe Jordan played for Morton, Leeds United, Manchester United, AC Milan, Verona, Southampton and Bristol City. Jordan had the distinction of scoring in 3 World Cup Finals; in 1974, 1978 and 1982. Would that in the twenty first century Scotland had that kind of forward line talent to choose from.

Archie McLean would have loved to witness that Scottish team, and their clash with Brazil in 1974 in Frankfurt.

One of the players to become prominent in the emergence of Brazilian football at the time Archie played, was a young man named Artur Friedenreich. He in fact played alongside McLean for various selects for the Paulista. The question Brazil was asking, was Artur a better player than the great Pele, in the debate, Fried versus Pele? Artur scored goals from season 1911, when he scored 4 goals for Germania, till season 1934, when aged forty two, he scored for Sao Paulo. In total he scored 355 goals for Paulista. He was born in 1892, and played as a winger and centre forward for six teams in the Sao Paulo area. He scored 1329 goals overall in his career. Artur is reckoned to have scored 45 more goals than Pele. Sadly, the records which Artur's father Oscar and later a team mate from Paulistano, Mario de Andrado had completed, vanished after Andrados' death in the mid 1960's.

Artur was the son of a German father and a Brazilian mother, and made a significant impact as the first coloured player to break through the early racial and cultural barriers in Brazilian football; he played 17 international games between 1914 and 1930, and scored 8 goals.

The Guinness Book of Records states under the heading most goals "in a specified period", the greatest number of goals scored is 1281 by the legendary Brazilian player Pele in 1363 games from 7 September 1956 to 1 October 1977. His thousandth goal came during his nine hundredth and ninety first class match on 19th November 1969, when he scored a penalty for his club Santos at the Maracano Stadium in Rio de Janeiro. Pele won 111 caps, and his final cap was in 1971. Pele announced his retirement at the end of the season 1974. His retirement was short lived, as the following year he signed a £2 million contract with the New York Cosmos, for whom he played till 1977, Pele became the first truly global sports personality, and it is doubtful if anyone will match his universal appeal.

Artur lived in a different era, but he prepared the way for future stars like Pele to be accepted world wide. Archie McLean was able to associate with and have a position of influence on players, who laid the foundation for the Brazilians future World Cup successes, such as Artur Friedenreich.

How Scotland could have done with fair players like Archie McLean, and have forward partnerships like the

McLean-Hopkins combination. After Scotland's last game in the World Cup in France 98 Gordon Strachan (in 2006 the Celtic manager) wrote on 29 June 1998, in The Observer, when he mourned the lack of flair players who were eligible to play for Scotland.
Strachan Wrote,

'Players from South America and Africa seem to get much greater encouragement to express themselves and take chances on the ball. You could argue that this is sometimes taken to extremes, and causes them to become vulnerable, but they recognise that even the well-organised defences are going to have problems in dealing with opponents who keep wanting to beat two or three players. One of the differences between Scotland and Morocco was that you had to look long and hard for anyone in a Scotland shirt to produce the unexpected. That is not to say Scotland has no particularly skilful players. John Collins is definitely in that category. But one or two in your team is not enough. If you're going to play with imagination, everybody must be on the same wavelength.
Sadly, from what I have seen of the Scotland under 21 team, I cannot offer much hope of a dramatic transformation in the near future. It has to be viewed as a long-term project and, for me, one of the keys lies in managers and coaches encouraging young players to follow the examples set by the South Americans and Africans. This will involve addressing how players are developed in Scotland, as schoolboy players and professionals. As a professional footballer myself, I was fortunate not to have received any formal football coaching until I was 13 or 14.

I just played, and concentrated on enjoying myself'.
John Collins played in the Scottish team in the World Cup games in France in 1998. He was quoted in the Observer on 14 June 1998, after Scotland had played Brazil on 10 June and were about to play Norway on 16 June.

'There will be more physical contact against Norway than against Brazil, I'm sure of that. The Brazilians have such terrific skill that it's hard to get tackles in. There's no space between them and the ball, so it's all about jockeying them. That was alien to us, but there's nothing like the same level of skill in the game, and that's why you see so many tackles being made week in, week out. This game against Norway will suit our guys much better; they'll see more of the ball'.

Yes, indeed there was a lack of flair players in 1998, and following on into the twenty first century Scotland still has this lack. In the spring of 2006, those who love football everywhere mourned the passing of the former Celtic player Jimmy Johnstone, winner of a European cup medal in 1967. How flair players like him are greatly missed so much in this new century. As other nations are developing flair players Scotland seems unable to produce anything more than very competitive journeymen.

PHOTOGRAPHS

The photographs included in this book have been made available courtesy of the following

PHOTOGRAPHY	COURTESY OF
Front Cover	- Barbara Key

The renovated Lonend Complex at Anchor Mill, now used as accommodation.

1.	Archie McLean	- Malcolm McLean
2.	Burnfoot House	- Claire Wadsworth
3.	Charles Miller Plaque	- Mara Gago
4.	Archie's Post Card	- Scottish Football Museum
5.	Coats Sao Paulo	- Mara Gago
6.	Sao Paulo Athletics Club	- John Mills
7.	The Consolation Cup	- Scottish Football Museum
8.	McLean's Home	- Mara Gago
9.	Pacaembu Stadium	- Mara Gago
10.	Archie's Medals	- Malcolm McLean
11.	The Bowl House and South Green At Anchor Bowling club in Paisley	- Claire Wadsworth
12.	The Beautiful Team 1970	- Paisley Express
13.	Families from Rue Jorge Morreira	- Nancy Watson (Nee McNeil)
14.	Bowls Team 1935	- Nancy Watson (Nee McNeil)
15.	Archie Gemmell	- SNS Group

Back Cover   Paisley Express

This Aerial photograph of the central area of Paisley shows Coats Mills in the background. The large building, near the river, on the right, has now been restored, and has been converted into flats (known as Lonend) The Mill Building on the far left is now used as offices (and known as Mile End)

Archie McLean photographed at Elderslie Golf Club near Paisley , wearing his hallmark bow-tie

Burnfoot House in the village of Fairlie in Ayrshire where John Miller, Charles Miller's father was born

The Plaque inside the Pacaembu Stadium commemorating Charles Miller

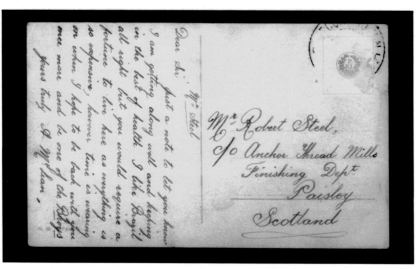

S. Paulo - Ponte Grande

Ediçao Malusardi

A Postcard sent from Brazil 1912 sent by Archie McLean to his works manager, Robert Steel at the Anchor Thread Mill in Paisley

**Main Entrance - Coats Corrente in Ipirango
area of Sao Paulo**

**The Sao Paulo Athletic Club in the Consolacao area of
Sao Paulo**

The Consolation Cup won in 1912 by Johnstone with Archie McLean

The home of McLean Family at 62,Rua Jorgi Morreira in the Ipirango area of Sao Paulo

The Pacaembu Stadium in Sao Paulo

**Archie received this medal in 1924, When his team won
the Bon Accord Cup**

The Bowls House and South Green at the Anchor Bowling Club in Paisley

'The Beautiful Team' who won the World Cup in Mexico in 1970 for Brazil

**Families from Coats Mills who lived in Rua Jorgi
Morriera, Sao Paulo, on the steps of the
Sao Paulo Athletics Club**

**Bowling in Sao Paulo in February 1935, includes,
Jack and Archie McLean,
Hector McNeil and Harry Hardaker**

**Archie Gemmill celebrating 'His Goal'
against Holland at Argentina 1978**

Eight

Archie McLean,
<u>The Forgotten Father of Brazilian Football</u>

On the 30 May 2006, Scottish television screened a half
hour programme, by way of the lead up to the 2006 World
Cup, which was to kick off on 9 June in Germany.
The programme title was 'Archie McLean: The Forgotten
Father of Brazilian Football'.
The programme opened by making the claim that Scotland
gave Brazil its samba style football, and showed the medals
and trophies which are displayed in the Scottish Football
Museum at Hampden Park. These were won in Sao Paulo,
Brazil by a little known Scottish footballer, who played for
Ayr and Johnstone in the early twentieth century.

    The focus then turned to Richard McBrearty, the
custodian at the Scottish Football Museum. He stated,
referring to Archie, 'Arriving in Brazil he soon set up a
football team called the Scottish Wanderers to play in the
local state league in Sao Paulo, the same league in which
Pele later played, with the Santos team . From the start,
Archie was a classic outside forward. Although very slight
in stature, Archie was quick, and the Brazilians liked to see
this kind of play'.

    Another thing which was important about McLean,
was the type of game he brought to Brazil, the classic short
passing game. He teamed up with an Englishman Bill
Hopkins, and the two of them played the short passing
game on the run.

Archie brought to Brazil, what the Brazilians called 'The Little Chart' way of playing, and what they meant, was that McLean and his team mates were plotting their course, the way a ship plots a course on a chart. This was very different to Brazilian football, and was something he gave to Brazilian football. Look what happened within a few years on the short passing game. Brazil went on to dominate world football.

Malcolm McLean, Archie's grandson then took centre stage in the programme and he said, 'I lived with Archie in Paisley during the school holidays. I got to know him really well. He was very modest, and very rarely talked about football. He would take me to football matches in Paisley to see St Mirren. He was a St Mirren supporter, and as we sat at the game, that was the only time he would tell me about some of his football experiences in Brazil. After he retired, he went to Brazil only once. He went to the stadium in Sao Paulo. He was introduced to the crowd and got a big ovation. He was really thrilled, and it came to him that he had achieved something in his past'.

Before retracing his grandfather's career in Brazil, Malcolm decided to visit the National Records Office at Colindale in London, where records go back 200 years. Malcolm was able to research Archie's football career, and find out just how he introduced a football style that lead to Brazilian football stars like Ronaldo entertaining millions. Malcolm went on to say 'I have made a fascinating discovery from a Brazilian newspaper which had a team photograph of a team called 'SC Americano' who played in the Local Paulisa (Sao Paulo) league. The article told that the team were to go to Argentina. What happened was that in the early days of international football in South America, Brazil took the best club side in the country, and sent them to play as representatives of Brazil. Archie was in the line up and was the only non Brazilian in the team'.

Malcolm went on to say, 'how thrilled I was, as he hadn't seen that particular photograph before, although I was aware of the team'.

Malcolm indicated he would take a copy, and treasure it as a keepsake'.

The programme then showed in Sao Paulo, the Charles Miller Square which was named after the man who brought football to Brazil in 1894. It went on to state that it wasn't till 18 years later that the famous style of samba football was introduced, when a certain Archie McLean arrived in Sao Paulo.

When Malcolm arrived in Sao Paulo, his first destination was the Ipiranga district, where Archie worked from 1912 at J and P Coats textile factory. Above the factory gate is the factory name 'Coats Carrente'.

The factory is still in operation in the twenty first century, as is the machinery Malcolm's grandfather worked on.

Mario Rodricho of Coats Sao Paulo, showed where Archie had worked, pointing out the drying processing and thread winding department of the factory. He went on to talk about how Archie and others had set up the Scottish Wanderers, and that they had played in the Paulista league. He told how Archie had inspired Brazilian football players to leave the long ball and kick and rush tactics behind. He talked about the locals, who were amazed as they watched the Scottish Wanderers, how a group of foreigners could move and pass with such flair. Mario reminded us that that Archie had quickly persuaded the Brazilians to abandon the long ball style, and work on skill and technique instead.

Malcolm next went on to visit the Sao Paulo Athletics Club (known as SPAC), where his guide was John Mills of SPAC. Malcolm was shown a team photograph from 1935, which showed both Archie and his son Robert (Malcolm's Father). Archie by then was long past his peak, but still enjoyed to play.

John stated that into the twenty first century, there is still talk of Archie's influence. He indicated that Archie had played for St Benedicten Gymnasium, the old boys and friends of St Benedicten School in the centre of Sao Paulo. Archie played there till 1920. John went on to mention that these were three of the main teams in Sao Paulo area.

1. Corinthians
2. Santos
3. Palmeiras

Three professional teams among the best in Brazil, have their roots in the league.

Scottish viewers watching this programme will find it mystifying that a guy called Archie McLean from Paisley taught the Brazilians how to play football. It is a fact that a hundred years ago, the British were the professors of football, and nations like Brazil were the pupils. How things have changed!

Malcolm then went to visit the home Archie and his wife had in Ipiranga district of Sao Paulo. It was owned by Coats and in 2006 was up for sale. The McLeans lived there from 1922 till 1949. The street was Rua Jorgi Moreira, and the house was number 62. It is a villa, and looks in great condition, even in the twenty first century. The commentary went on to say that 'some football historians believe many Brazilian legends we have become familiar with over the years, simply wouldn't have had the chance to shine, if it wasn't for the intelligence of Archie McLean'.

A World Cup winner for Brazil Juninho who had played for Celtic, and is now with the Sao Paulo Club Palmeiras, is one of the few Brazilian players who had a success in British football, and knows the influence the Scots had. He was asked about this, and as to how Brazilian football had developed so much. He commented as follows; 'Well, I think you will find wherever you go in the city of Sao Paulo, you will see young boys playing football in any open space'.

When asked, "Do you think Brazilians would be surprised by the Scottish influence in the game they love so much?"

Juninho's response was 'I really think as it is you bring together the best football in the world, with the fast game played in Europe, and the skills and technique of South America. This is the best way to play football'.

The focus then turned to Aidan Hamilton, who had written the book 'An Entirely Different Game' about the British influence on Brazilian football. This book contained a chapter entitled 'Wanderers from Scotland'.

Aidan discussed the fact that Archie and an English player Bill Hopkins, who played along side him, were inventors of 'Tabelinha', (one-two) which in Portuguese literally means the 'Little Chart'. It described an interpassing move involving two players.

Aidan, whose book outlined the British influence on Brazilian football, believed 'Archie's influence lives on in the way the game is played.'

'Archie tried to install discipline in the way the game was played, and this was illustrated by an incident when a couple of players wanted to see how high they could kick the ball. McLean soon put a stop to that'.

In the early 1940's the commentator, journalist and football coach Max Valentine produced a work entitled 'Football and Technique', where he cited Archie's influence. This influence can be traced to be more than that of Charles Miller, who was mainly remembered as an organiser of football in Brazil back in the1890's. Aidan considered that Archie's legacy can be seen today by the way Roberto Carlos interacted with Ronaldinho.

The focus then turned to Fleminense Football Club. They have a small ground capacity of 8000 at the Larenjeiras Football stadium in Rio de Janeiro. Archie had played and scored goals at this ground in 1910, 1914 and 1916 as he represented Sao Paulo's state team.

Malcolm McLean commented that it was great to stand on the same pitch his grandfather had played on. He was impressed by the stadium's great atmosphere, and it hadn't changed that much since Archie played there. Malcolm stated that Archie played the most important games of his career in the Larenjeiras Stadium with the Sao Paulo state team, in their games against the Rio state team. Malcolm went on to say it felt great.

Many pictures of Archie can be found in the Fleminese archives called Flu-Memoria, which is a treasure trove of football nostalgia from the twentieth century. The Curator Louis Feraira recognised the importance of Archie, and he said, 'McLean was very important, indeed yes, he played at Fluminese for the Paulista team, and was one of the key players of the 1910's'. Among the memorabilia, was an after match dinner menu which all the players involved signed, including Archie.

At the Archives was a programme for a game in 1914, which showed Archie, Bill Hopkins and Artur Friedenreich. Artur played at centre forward, with Archie and Bill playing on his left.

The commentary went on to remark on the fact that a lad from Paisley was involved in all of this. Malcolm commented that he felt it was incredible that records exist in Brazil, but in Scotland no one knows anything about him. He hoped that would change in the future.

The programme then focused on Roberta Asis, who is a well known football pundit in Brazil. He went on to say; 'Archie created the idea of a wing where two players played in harmony, as he and Bill Hopkins did. This was something new in, Brazil. Brazil learned much from the position Archie played in, and this was important for 'Brazilian football'.

The programme concluded that Archie had worked in Brazil for nearly forty years. Hence his grandson

Malcolm had the opportunity to learn the real story of a man to whom the Brazilians owe much, but little is known of him in his native Scotland. In just a few days, his journey allowed Malcolm to meet people who knew more of Archie McLean's football life than he did.
Malcolm was able to expand his knowledge and his feelings for Archie during the time in he spent in Brazil. This is where his grandfather had worked , where his social life had been, his football life, with the status he had in the game he loved, both in Sao Paulo and further a field in Brazil.

The author would like to acknowledge the help of STV in allowing him to quote from their television programme *Archie McLean- The Forgotten Father of Brazilian Football.*

Nine

What the papers have said

For nearly a hundred years Archie McLean has featured in newspaper articles in Scotland. Quite an achievement for any footballer , especially one who gained his fame in an other country, and is relatively unknown in Scotland in the twenty-first century .

From the Ayr Observer and Galloway Chronicle November 16, 1909, under the heading 'Chats with favourite footballers A. McLean Ayr FC'.
Archie related how he came to join Ayr FC.' It was just after the Fair holidays (the Paisley trades holiday fortnight is the first two weeks in August), "I had just got home and into bed and I was woken up and told that a director of Ayr FC was waiting for me. Out I went to the door, and then I was signed on".
McLean went on to tell 'I started with a Barrhead team and played for Arthurlie, (Arthurlie in the twenty first century are a successful Junior team with a ground in Barrhead), and I was with them when their pavilion got burned down.

After that I went to Bute Athletic, and while with them I was supposed to have got my cap against England. I had won my cap in the trials between Renfrewshire and Ayrshire, but through some misunderstanding, my Junior International cap went elsewhere. I played for Woolwich Arsenal, (now just know as Arsenal) when they were touring Scotland, and I was included in the games against Raith Rovers and Aberdeen. I did not get an offer from the

Arsenal, but Celtic and Hibs wanted me, and just after I
had fixed up with Ayr, Hibs came after me again.'
This interview took place after Ayr FC had just won a local
derby against the other Ayr team Parkhouse. When he was
asked about his other sporting activities, he replied 'well I
used to do a bit at high jumping and I've a badge for a 5'1"
jump. Then I'm fond of billiards and a keen cyclist'.
Archie then concluded by saying 'I should have told them I
played for Perthshire, (that's Glasgow Perthshire, a Junior
team that played and still does so at Maryhill in Glasgow).
I had some terrible times for the ground is so hard I was
forever getting cut and hacked by falling'.

From the Paisley and Renfrewshire Gazette dated
November 9, 1913. This was a letter to the editor from
R.R, under the heading "Coats football team in Brazil",
reporting on the Scottish Wanderers in Sao Paulo.
Sir,
Last week we opened our new ground, which, although just
on the small side, was presented to us by a Syrian
gentleman here, and we played a club called the Orient F.C.
It was rather an auspicious opening, as near the end of the
game, when we were leading by 12-2, the Orient players
were getting annoyed at our passing game and started to
hustle a bit. One of their players made straight for our
outside-left with the intention of laying him low, but he
came off second best. Instead of taking it, he made off for
our pavilion, returning with a knife. In a few minutes there
were five or six knifes on the job, but before they knew
there were a few Scotch fists were being put hard on their
faces. The Scottish Wanderer who really infuriated the

oriental players was the outside left namely Archie McLean with his dribbling and trickery.

This timely action had effect and in a minute there was a hasty retreat of the blood-seekers, they having had quite enough, as they say here of the "Systema Inglez" and we left the field victors in the football by 12 to 2.

Although knives seem to be in the outfit of that particular club, I do not wish you to think all the other clubs here are alike, as in the other matches we have played the clubs acted in a sportsmanlike way and the games were very enjoyable.

Some kick-offs are rather early, such as 7.15am, but this is to escape the heat of the day-but I will not say what "day" as most of the players have friends in your town, and they might get a shock to think of them playing on that particular day.

We get fairly good "gates" at our matches, but we need all the money, as expenses are very high, a ball itself costing £1 7s 6d.

I must close now as I am afraid the secretaries of the local football clubs might be offering terms to some of our players if I say any more about the "Scottish Wanderers" – yours etc' R.R

This Systema Inglesa (English System) was begun by a Scot Jock Hamilton from Ayr, who had played for Fulham. Jock became the first professional football coach, coaching the Sao Paulo team Paulistano. This system is still used, and should have been called the Scottish System, but the locals did not know the difference between Scotland and England.

From the Times of Brazil dated June 7, 1963.
"Back home in Paisley Archie McLean still plays golf four times a week (at the Elderslie Golf club just West of Paisley). When Archie is not golfing he plays bowls (at the Anchor Bowling Club which is associated with the Anchor Mill in the Seedhill Area in the East End of Paisley)."
The article went on to point out that during Archie's time in Brazil, he had witnessed no less than four revolutions.
Archie attended International games and watched the national side play against Austria earlier in 1963. He was interested by Scotland's performance.

Neil Stuart wrote in 1965 about the challenges in communication St Mirren had with their new Brazilian player Fernando Azevedo. They called on Archie McLean to help out, when they were important matters to discuss with Fernando. This allowed him to keep up to speed with Portuguese, and so be able to help, when communication between the St Mirren management and Ferdinand got difficult.
Neil went on to refer to the fact that Archie played for Brazilian Selects in the same position as Pele did, including playing in the same number 10 shirt.

Archie won several tennis and bowling championships in Sao Paulo, and was an accomplished golfer and swimmer.

In the Daily Record dated Wednesday June 24 1970, in an article written by Len Findlay, under the heading 'The Scot Who Taught The World Champions'.
On Sunday June 21st 1970, Brazil won the World Cup for the third time, and with this win, they took ownership of

the Jules Rimet Trophy, which was the supreme prize in football. Len Findlay interviewed Archie McLean at the Anchor Bowling Green, in the shadow of where Archie had worked way back 60 years ago in the Anchor Mill.

When Archie arrived in Brazil in 1912, he thought he was going to be living and working in Rio. In fact when the ship he was on arrived there, football officials tried to sign him to play in Rio, but Archie was bound for Sao Paulo.

During his football career in Sao Paulo, he played in representative matches against a team from Rio, and Archie indicated that there was as much rivalry as between Celtic and Rangers.

Through Archie's efforts, the locals started to develop a game with lots of passing movements, revolutionising the way football was played in Brazil. Although not well known or acknowledged in his native Scotland, Archie became a national hero in Brazil. He met the president, and was treated with great honour and respect. When Pele and the rest of the "beautiful team" were dazzling their way to a third World Cup win, Archie, who now lived in Ralston in the Paisley area, had the opportunity to reflect on wonderful memories, and have a great sense of pride at the Brazilian team's achievements.

In less than a year after watching Brazil's World Cup triumph on TV, Archie passed away. The following notice appeared in the Paisley Express:

McLean – at the Royal Alexandra Infirmary Annexe, on 31st May 1971. Archibald Fulton McLean 47 of Atholl Crescent (formerly of Sao Paulo, Brazil), beloved husband

of the late Margaret McNeil. Funeral tomorrow
Wednesday, friends desirous of attending please meet at
Woodside Crematorium at 3.30pm. No flowers or letters
please.

In the Daily Mail on Friday December 18th, 1998
Brian Scott in his column 'At Large with Brian Scott' under
the headlines.
'Scot who sent Brazil football daft – Brian Scott
investigates the curious case of the first samba star.
Curious talk of a Scotsman in South America'.
Brian Scott talks about Archie McLean being one of the
great names in Brazilian Football's Hall of Fame, and about
the references to Archie in Aiden Hamilton's book 'An
Entirely different game'.
Aiden quotes from a publication by the St Andrew's
Society of Sao Paulo.
"Archie McLean is revered in Brazilian sporting circles.
When he made a sentimental return to Brazil in 1966 he
received a standing ovation from a large group of
spectators who were at a game in the Pacaembu Stadium."
The article as discussed by Aiden Hamilton, goes on to talk
about the influence of Charles Miller, whose father was
Scottish,

A book on the history of football quoting directly from
Brian Scott's article in his adopted country testifies:
'MacLean (sic) was an artist, a worthy exponent of the
Scottish School. His scientific football became more
prominent when he formed a partnership on the left wing
with an Englishman called Bill Hopkins'.
'That left wing was a machine'.

McLean and Bill Hopkins, apparently shared a telepathic understanding. Their passing gave rise to a term known even today as Tabelinha or Little Chart. The two were the only non-Brazilians to play against Chile and Argentina in the mid-1910s shortly after the formation of the Brazilian FA.

McLean, playing his Brazilian club football initially with the Scottish Wanderers, who were made up exclusively of Coats' workers, represented the Paulistas regularly, from 1914 to 1924, by which time he would be verging on 37years old .

His is a fascinating tale, one that is treasured by his grandson, Malcolm McLean, who was born in Brazil before being sent to boarding school in Dollar, and electing to stay in Scotland after studying at University here.

'My grandfather had returned to Paisley by the time I came to school in this country,' says Malcolm, now 50, and an architect in Glasgow.

'I used to stay with him during the school holidays, so knew him very well. It's just regrettable now that he never sat me down and told me all about his football in Brazil. He told me bits and pieces, of course, and I do have a few cuttings from newspapers about him. I know, too, that he greatly admired the more modern Brazilian players, and took some pride from having preceded them. The fact that he played inside-left, Pele's position, is a nice association'.

In the Scottish Daily Mail on 27 June 2002 an exclusive article by Gavin Madelly had as its headlines. Revealed: Scot who made it possible for Argentina to take England today, a son of the Clyde who became the father of Argentinean football. Some people are aware that Argentine football started with immigrant teams, but most people will be surprised to discover the first ever president of the country's football association was a son of the Clyde, namely Alexander Watson Hutton, usually known as Watson Hutton. Hutton's remarkable life began in Glasgow, on June 10, 1853, both his parents having died when he was young. He was educated at Daniel Stewart's Hospital School in Edinburgh, before matriculating at Edinburgh University in 1872, at the age of 19 years. He graduated with a Second class M.A in Philosophy, but the deaths of two brothers from tuberculosis may have prompted his decision, on doctor's advice, to leave Scotland for a better climate. He arrived in Buenos Aires in 1881, to take up the post of headmaster at the St Andrew's School, which ministered to the educational needs of the Argentine capital's sizeable Scottish congregation.

Hutton's enthusiasm for football led him to set up the country's first national league in 1891, and all five teams in that league were made up entirely of British players. Locals would look on in bemusement, as the 'loco' foreigners chased a ball around a field in the searing midday heat.

The Argentine Association Football League evolved into the Argentine FA in 1903, and Hutton was appointed the Association's first president. In 1898, he founded his own senior club, Alumni, which was full of his former school-boys, to play in the new Argentine League. It was dominated by members of one Scottish family, the Browns, and his own son, Arnoldo Pencliffe Watson Hutton.

The Alumni went on to win the league championship ten times in 12 years, and their players formed the backbone of the national side. On June 12th, 1910, an Argentine side featuring Jorge Gibson Brown, Ernesto Alejandro Brown and Arnolodo Watson Hutton beat Uruguay 4-1. But, by 1913, British influence was finally waning in the national side, and home grown talent started seeping into the league. However, in some ways, the British hold over the Argentinian game has never faded. It hasn't occurred to anybody to change the utterly English names of so many leading clubs – River Plate, Racing or Newells Old Boys, (where the 2002 coach, Marcelo Bielsa, began his career).

Interestingly, the Browns link with the national side has also survived into modern times. One descendent, also called James Brown, played alongside Diego Maradona in the 1986 World Cup final against Germany. Alexander Watson Hutton died in Buenos Aires on March 9, 1936, less than six years after his adopted country reached the first ever world cup final. But his name lives on with the library of the Argentine FA named after him. It is a fitting tribute to his learned contribution to world football.

Jed O'Brien who was formally the director and founder of the Scottish Football Museum, had stated that three men all with strong Scottish connections were responsible for the development of football in South America. It would appear that these three men were:

- Charles Miller
- Archie McLean
- Watson Hutton

This article appeared in the newspaper on the day England played against Argentina in the 2002 world cup finals. Four years earlier in France, Argentina had beaten England with David Beckham being red carded. The 2002 result went England's way, allowing them to progress to play against Brazil. They lost and Brazil went on to win the World Cup for the fifth time.

In the Daily Record which is published in Glasgow in January 25 2005 edition, Brian McIver writing under the heading of 'Pass Master Scot who taught Brazilians how to play the beautiful game'. stated that
'Archie McLean preceded Pele, Zico and Jairzinho as a legend in Brazilian football. Archie's legend, according to McIver, was that he managed to refine natural skill, and add the short basic game that would bring Brazil in 2002, their fifth world cup success. Archie is quoted as saying of his team-mates 'they were great players but terribly undisciplined, their antics would not have been tolerated in Scotland'.

Richard McBrearty of the Scottish Football Museum said 'Archie McLean is one of the most important figures in football history in Brazil and Scotland. He introduced them to the style of play for which Brazilians are now famous around the world. It is about time that he got the recognition he deserves in his native land'.

n Times Online dated 23 January 2005 under the heading 'Connery to film the Scot who gave Brazil football'.
The article stated that Archie McLean is credited with being the 'Father of Brazilian Football'.

Karen Goodwin who penned the article, described McLean
as one of the original 'Samba Stars', and his incredible
story will be told in a television documentary with Sean
Connery, which will be screened by the BBC in 2007.
Connery was a keen amateur player who at one point
turned down the opportunity to join Manchester United.
He became fascinated by Archie's story while working on a
series that will explore Scottish culture with Murray
Grigor, who is an independent film maker, formerly a
director of the Edinburgh Film Festival. Alex Ferguson,
the Manchester United manager, was able to tell Connery
all about Archie. He was nicknamed O'Veadinol – the
little deer, which was the name given to a street in Sao
Paulo.

McLean returned to Sao Paulo for a visit in 1966. He
was guest of honour at a match in the city's Pacaembu
football stadium, and given a rousing reception.
The article quoted Jed O'Brien of the Scottish Football
Museum at Hampden Park in Glasgow, Jed stated 'He
took the passing and running game of football to Brazil.
The genius of the national team, which is one of the best in
the world, is directly attributable to McLean and the
Scottish Wanderers. There should be a 20ft statue to him in
Paisley yet sadly most people today will have not heard of
him. We are so used to the official history that tells us the
English brought football to Brazil'.

On a more local basis Derek Parker wrote an article in
the Paisley Daily Express dated Thursday February 8,
2005. The two page spread had its heading.
'Film will celebrate the amazing life of Archie McLean –

The Buddie Who Taught Brazilians the Beautiful Game'
Screen star Sean Connery is just the man to play The Little
Deer. The article focused on Archie's farewell from Sao
Paulo, when he received a silver salver from Harold Spain
of the Sao Paulo Athletics Club. Archie and his wife
Margaret were able to celebrate fifty years of marriage with
golden wedding celebrations 22nd October 1960.

From the Paisley Daily Express Thursday May 25
2006 under the heading, 'Modest Buddie was the father of
modern Brazilian Football'.
TV programme charted Archie McLean's lasting influence
on the beautiful game. The paper gave over pages 12 and
13 to an article penned by Frank Hurley. Frank wrote, As
Brazilian soccer stars Samba their way through the World
Cup finals in Germany next month June 2006, Scotland can
console itself that although we didn't qualify we will be
there in spirit. Skilful Brazilian players of the twenty-first
century, such as Ronaldinho, Ronaldo, Kaka and the rest of
the squad, they wouldn't be able to display their mesmeric
football skills, if it wasn't for a Buddie who taught them
how to play the Beautiful Game.
When Paisley's Archie McLean landed on the shores of
Brazil 94 years ago, little did he know that he was about to
revolutionise the way the locals played football by
introducing them to the Scottish style of football.
He was to become the father of Brazilian football – revered
in that country but an unknown prophet in his own land.
The dapper textile mill engineer kicked the long ball the
Brazilians played into touch and showed them how to
dribble and keep possession with short passes, to carve up

an opponents defence.

The Brazilians natural ability and McLean's quiet determination transformed their game into the style that has since astonished football fans across the globe.

Yet McLean is only now getting the recognition he deserves in his homeland for his massive contribution, which historians say led to the creation of the style of the world's greatest Brazilian players such as Pele and Garrincha.

In Brazil, his memory is revered not only by footballers, but by legions of soccer fans.

In Scottish Television's documentary, Archie McLean – The Forgotten Father of Brazilian Football – viewers will learn his incredible life story. What better person to follow in the footballing legend's steps than his grandson, Malcolm McLean, who has fond boyhood memories of his granddad, who finally returned home to Paisley in 1949 ?

Malcolm, 57, an architect, spent his early years growing up in Brazil with his parents. He returned to the UK, and was boarded at rugby playing Dollar Academy, near Stirling. But on holidays, he stayed with his granddad in Paisley. Malcolm said he played amateur football at Strathclyde University in Glasgow, and wished his school had been football orientated – not rugby.

He told the Paisley Daily Express: 'My granddad was a season ticket holder at St Mirren until the day he died. He was a very modest man, yet it was at Love Street matches that he gradually talked to me about his playing days in Brazil, and I got the first inkling of what he had achieved'.

'Quite literally, granddad taught the Brazilians how to play football the way Scots did back home'.

'The Brazilians played the long ball game, booting it up the park'.

'Grandad showed them how to make short passes and dribble the ball, keep possession and chart a way through the defence'.

'What is absolutely amazing about his story is that he gets whole chapters in Brazil's history books and sporting pages'.

'Yet in Scotland very few know about his footballing exploits'.

'I bet a lot of people in Paisley who are St Mirren supporters haven't a clue about his achievements in Brazil'.

'I've spoken to very senior players in Brazil and they regard Grandad as a very important person who was vitally important in shaping the game'.

Soon his life would be transformed from wet and windy West of Scotland, to the steamy heat in Brazil, when, in 1912, he was transferred to a factory in Sao Paulo, Brazil. It was in his spare time, that the canny Scot noticed the Brazilians played a very traditional game of booting the ball down the park and chasing after it.

But they lacked possession, and vital dribbling skills, of which he was a master. Archie's football career flourished, and he was selected to play for high profile Brazilian teams like SC Americano, Sao Bento and Sao Paulo Athletic Club.

Archie had planned to stay in Brazil for three months, but stayed for nearly forty years. Along with other expatriate employees at the company's Brazilian plant, he set up a football team called the Scottish Wanderers, who played in blue shirts and white shorts.

The team competed in a number of friendly fixtures, and it wasn't long before the talented dribbler and short ball passer was being invited to turn out for Brazilian teams like Sao Paulo Athletic Club, Sao Bento and SC Americano, winning several league titles and cups along the way.

His talents soon earned him selection for the Paulista League team – the second highest accolade in Brazilian football, after playing for the national side.

He persuaded the Brazilians to work on skills, and introduced a short passing game on the run. The style formed the basis of modern Brazilian football, which has won several World Cups and produced soccer stars like Pele, Garrincha, Cesar, Jairzinho, Ronaldinho and Rivaldo. In the fascinating documentary, Malcolm's journey takes him from the National Records Office in London to Sao Paulo.

Brazilians play football differently. Its essence is a game in which prodigious individual skills outshine team tactics, where dribbles and flicks are preferred over physical challenges or long distance passes.

Perhaps because of the emphasis on the dribble, which moves one's whole body, Brazilian football is often described in musical terms – in particular as a 'samba.'

In his search for Archie's life story, Malcolm meets World Cup winner Juninho, who plays for Sao Paulo team Palmeries; author Aiden Hamilton, who has written a book about British influence on Brazilian football; and John Mills of Sao Paulo Athletics Club, where Archie was a member for nearly 40 years.

Malcolm added: 'Archie was a modest man and rarely talked about his football career, so the trip was full of fascinating discoveries for me. I felt really proud to have known him'.

A lifelong fitness enthusiast, Archie became a member of Paisley's Anchor Bowling Club and Elderslie Golf Club on his return to Scotland.

Sadly, he passed away in 1971, aged 84.

At her home in Atholl Crescent, Ralston, where Archie spent the final years of his life, Barbara, Malcolm's mum, remembered him as a proud but quiet man, who never went out without being smartly dressed, wearing his trademark Kelly bow tie. The Scottish Football Museum honours Archie in their football history displays.

In Paisley there's nothing to commemorate one of the town's greatest human exports.

The most recent newspaper article on Archie McLean was in The Scotsman of 30th May 2006 by James Gilchrist under the heading 'The Scot who gave Brazil the most beautiful game of all'. In the article James Gilchrist, gave a summary of the STV programme on Archie McLean which was screened on the 30th May 2006.

Ten

Honouring a Buddy

Charles Miller had a statue erected in his honour. As his funeral procession passed a football match which was in progress, the game stopped as a mark of respect. Throughout Brazil, even those who have no great love or interest in futebol are able to say that Charles Miller, started football while still a teenager. There was even a street named after him in Brazil. In comparison, Archie McLean's contribution was widely acknowledged in the Sao Paulo area of Brazil, and throughout the country, but there was little awareness in Scotland of his contribution to Brazilian football for many years. It is reported that after his return to Scotland, Archie made a visit back to Sao Paulo, where he was warmly applauded, and recognised more than thirty years after he had hung up his boots.

Over the years, there have been in the Scottish press, various articles about Archie's time in Brazil. In his book Aiden Hamilton devotes a chapter to the 'Wanderer from Scotland', with focus on Archie McLean. Paisley Museum mounted an exhibition on Archie's life and contributions. Renfrewshire Council's Museum Department, in conjunction with the Scottish Football Museum at Hampden Park, prepared the dialogue for the displays, and the staff at the museum prepared the displays. The exhibition was a popular attraction, and opened the eyes of a lot of 'buddies', as the town folk of Paisley are called, to Archie McLean, the footballer ambassador from their town.

THE ARCHIE McLEAN
EXIBITION
AT
PAISLEY MUSEUM

The Displays
- Archie McLean Footballer
- A Season of Two Halves
- 'An Artist, a Hero, A Most Loveable Scot'

Details of each of the displays in the exhibition are included, and an outline detailing the photograph which have been displayed in bold. The exhibition was a great success, but still Archie McLean was not a well known name in the greater Paisley area.

Archie McLean:
Footballer

When Archibald Fulton McLean was born at No 1 Dovesland, Paisley, on 11th July 1886, his father, John, and mother, Jane, would surely have been amazed to hear that their son, in the years to come, would spend nearly forty years in Brazil, where he would be hailed as a sporting hero.

Archie's father, brother and two elder sisters were already working in the Paisley Threadmills when he was born and Archie, too, began his working life unadventurously in Paisley.

Everything changed for him in June 1912, when he was sent to the Coats & Clarks mill at

Sao Paulo, Brazil, on what was originally meant to be a short term, temporary contract.

Clarks Anchor Thread Mill
Paisley June 1887

The Company had established a small mill in Brazil in 1908. A large mill was built at Ipiranga Sao Paulo , and in operation by 1910. Staff, mainly from Ferguslie, were sent out in twos and threes to train the Brazilian workers in the processes of spinning, twisting, hand-winding and finishing.

Workers and staff of the finishing department
at Ipiranga mill about 1913,

Work may have taken Archie to Brazil in 1912, but it was his football skills, and enthusiasm for the game, which were to make him famous in his adopted home. Somehow, he had found the time and energy to combine a promising football career with his work at the Mill. He took with him to Brazil the satisfaction of a successful and memorable season just completed.

Employees of J&P Coats with
their families at Sao Paulo during
Archie's early years in Brazil

A Season of Two Halves

Archie McLean had already played several seasons for teams such as Arthurlie, Glasgow Perthshire and Ayr FC, when he played his first game for Johnstone FC on 9th September 1911. The season started badly for the club. Early dismissal from the Scottish Qualifying Cup, before Archie had arrived, threatened the club with financial ruin. A run of defeats discouraged the supporters – on one occasion only one supporter travelled to an 'away' game. Archie himself, through praised as the team's most valuable newcomer, was felt to lack the robustness to play on bad pitches in difficult conditions.

**The back court at
Barclay Street, Paisley
where Archie lived as a boy.**

With the coming of 1912, Johnstone's football fortunes began to change, and Archie's with them. Notice was taken of his scoring spree of six goals in four games – not bad for a winger – his speed and cleverness on the ball and, particularly, his skilful combination play with his inside forward.

**A studio portrait
Of Archie and Margaret
McLean before 1912.**

The New Year brought early success for Johnstone against local rivals Arthurlie in the final of Renfrewshire's Victoria Cup, and a successful run in the Union League. Best of all, was a 2-1 victory in the Scottish Consolation Cup against Galston FC.

At the beginning of June, the club received the welcome news that their application for admission to the Second Division of the Scottish League had been accepted. Archie McLean, though, who had done so much to ensure their success, would not be there to help them. Archie was going to Brazil.

**Johnstone F.C. Team who
Won the Victoria Cup
1910-11 and
the Consolation Cup 1911-12**

"An Artist, A Hero, A Most Loveable Scot".
Archie's enthusiasm for football had an immediate impact, when he arrived at Sao Paulo in 1912. He took the lead establishing a football club, the 'Scottish Wanderers' and before long a piece of waste ground had been levelled to provide a pitch. Most of the players were from Paisley and worked at Ipiranga Mill.

**Scottish Wanderers at Sao Paulo in1912.
The team had strong Paisley
connections and included
Archie McLean**

His skill at the traditional Scottish short passing game was a revelation to the Brazilians. He went on to play for a number of Brazilian clubs and struck up a famous partnership with Bill Hopkins, a team-mate since the 'Scottish Wanderers' days, and with Artur Friedenrich, the greatest goal scorer and arguably the greatest player ever. Archie was a consistently prominent player and goal scorer among such exalted company and played in the matches between the representative teams of the Rio de Janeiro and Sao Paulo state leagues – the biggest games at this time, before full international matches began in South America. The forward line of Formiga, Demosthenes, Friedenrich, McLean and Hopkins was the best in Brazil at the time.

**Archie McLean with his
Americano Club team mates.**

Archie McLean on the extreme right, front row, with his Americano club team-mates. Archie helped the club to retain the Sao Paulo league trophy in 1913 and played in the side which achieved a notable draw against a visiting XI from Chile.

He played at the highest level during the formative years of the development of football in Brazil, earning for himself the affectionate nickname of 'Veadinho' or 'little deer'. He richly deserved his status as football hero in the world's greatest football nation.

Sao Paulo State Team with McLean and Hopkins

Could this be a question for some football or sports quiz in a Scottish pub ? Name a Scottish football player not in the Scottish Hall of Fame at Hampden Park, but is in some other Nation's Hall of Fame. On Monday 8th, November 2004 Dennis Law the former Manchester United player opened the Scottish Football Association' s Hall of Fame at Hampden Park   Scottish football supporters from across the world nominated players and managers to be inducted in the first group to be honoured. Then a panel of experts chose 20 from the names submitted and the following twenty Scots were inducted into the hall of heroes and referred to 'as inductees'. The main club(s) the inductees were associated with, is indicated beside their name.

Willie Woodburn	Rangers
Bobby Murdoch	Celtic
Jim Baxter	Rangers
Jimmy Johnstone	Celtic
Sir Alex Ferguson	Manchester United
Sir Matt Busby	Manchester United
Graeme Souness	Liverpool

Billy Bremner	Leeds United
John Greig	Rangers
Dave Mackay	Hearts & Tottenham Hotspur
Jock Stein	Celtic
Denis Law	Manchester United
Bill Shankley	Liverpool
Gordon Smith	Hibernian
Billy McNeil	Celtic
Willie Miller	Aberdeen
Jimmy McGrory	Celtic
Hughie Gallacher	Chelsea
Danny McGrain	Celtic
Kenny Dalglish	Celtic and Liverpool

This is the order the name have been presented as shown above.

The answer to the pub quiz question is Archie McLean, a number of Scots are in the National Football Hall of Fame at Preston, but they all have been inducted into the Scottish Hall of Fame.

There is no doubt that this list causes arguments among football supporters and pundits. Why no George Young or Lawrie Reilly or John White? Arguments may also focus on the value of discussion on the fact that 'these just don't make 'em like that any more'.

In the twenty first century Scotland does not have world class footballers of the calibre of Denis Law, Kenny Dalglish or Jim Baxter, although these players didn't bring Scotland the world cup success the nation craves for.

After qualifying for five successive World Cup finals, the

class of 2006 can't even do that, and are not likely to do so in the near future. Subsequent to expressing disappointment that George Young, Lawrie Reilly and John White were not in the hall of fame, a further 11 'inductees' were added to the hall of fame in November 2005.

They are:

Alan Morton	Rangers
Joe Jordan	Leeds United & ManchesterUnited
Alex McLeish	Aberdeen
John White	Totenham Hotspur
Bobby Lennox	Celtic
Lawrie Reilly	Hibernian
Charles Campbell	Queens Park
Willie Waddell	Rangers
George Young	Rangers
Alex James	Arsenal
Jim McLean	Dundee United

The Hall of Fame at the Scottish Football Museum is to honour players, managers and officials, who have reached the pinnacle of their profession and have made a significant contribution to Scotland's football reputation, through their spirit and determination.

More inductees will be added to the hall of fame before the end of 2006. The names of Archie McLean and Alexander Hutton should be candidates to be considered for this honour. No doubt there would be those who would ask, who are Archie McLean and Alexander Hutton, in the same way as those who will be asking who is Charles Campbell. Charles was born about 1850 and died in 1927. He started a sixteen year playing career with Queens Park as an amateur. He made 13 appearances for Scotland, and captained the team 8 times. He played in the F.A Cup Final twice with Queen's Park. Later he became president of Queen's Park, and subsequently President of the Scottish Football Association. In 1889 he refereed the Scottish Cup final. Charles Campbell played in the nineteenth century. He was the only hall of fame inductee so far , not to have played his football or managed a team in the twentieth century.

The Hall of Fame at the Scottish Football Museum as at 2006, only has as inductees players who have been eligible to play for Scotland, and managers who were or are Scots. The National Football Museum is located at the Preston North End Ground. The first National Football Museum hall of fame annual award' ceremony was held in December 2002. At that time 22 players and 6 managers were honoured.

The selection criteria for consideration for inclusion in the National Football Museum Hall of Fame are as follows:-

1.   A player must have either played in England for the majority of his career or played in England at least five seasons

2.   A manager or coach must have either managed or coached in England for the majority of his career, or managed or coached in England for at least five seasons,

and also either have retired from playing, or be over the age of 30 years.

The Scots in the National Football Museum Hall of Fame who are also in the Scottish Hall of Fame.

Alex James	Denis Law
Matt Busby	Billy Bremner
Bill Shankley	Kenny Dalglish
Dave Mackay	Alex Ferguson

The National Football Hall of Fame has 62 inductees as at the end of 2005 and includes besides Scots, players from Wales, Northern Ireland and Ireland. It also includes non British players such as Peter Schmeichel, Eric Cantona and also four women, Lily Parr, Sue Lopez, Debbie Bampton and Hope Powell.

The selection Panel included four sirs, Sir Bobby Charlton, Sir Alex Ferguson, Sir Tom Finney and Sir Trevor Brooking, who is the only one still to be inducted.

As far as the Scottish Hall of Fame is concerned, should stars of Scottish football such as Henrik Larsson be inducted? To date only Scots have been included but maybe because of the Graeme Souness revolution which started in the 1980's with Terry Butcher and others making such an impact on Scottish football, consideration should be given to extending the scope for those to be considered for the Scottish Hall of Fame.

On 12 November 2006, at the Thistle Hotel in Glasgow, the

06' group of 'inductees' to the Hall of Fame were introduced.

Would Terry Butcher, or Julie Fleeting (to acknowledge women's football), be among the inductees?

Those inducted to the Scottish Football Museums Hall of Fame for 06' were

Richard Gough	Rangers
Billy Steel	Morton and Derby County
Brian Laudrup	Rangers
Willie Ormond	Hibernian
Henrik Larsson	Celtic
John Robertson	Nottingham Forest
Davie Cooper	Rangers
Tommy Walker	Hearts
Tommy Gemmell	Celtic
Willie Henderson	Rangers
Sandy Jardine	Rangers and Hearts

The exciting aspect of the latest list of 'inductee', was inclusion of two foreigners to be voted into the elite band. Brian Laudrup who had played with Rangers was a Dane, and Henrik Larsson who had scored so many goals for Celtic was from Sweden.

On the basis of this development in some future years, Terry Butcher, Julie Fleeting and Archie McLean may be voted onto the Scottish Football Museum's Hall of Fame. In Britain, on television in the twenty first century, there are constantly programmes with a selection of a 'hundred best this or that' which can lead to all kinds of debate. If a poll was taken on the five most memorable events associated with Scottish football in the twentieth century, maybe the top five would be as follow, not in any chronological or significant order:

1. Celtic's European Cup victory in 1967.
2. Ranger's European Cup winners cup triumph of 1972.
3. Aberdeen's lifting of the same trophy in Gothenburg in 1983.
4. The victory by Scotland over World Cup winners England in 1967.
5. Archie Gemmill's goal against Holland in Argentina in the world cup in 1978.

Of these 5 events, four were very much team efforts, where as the fifth was to a large measure, an individual effort by another son of Paisley. Archie Gemmill was born in Paisley in March 1947. Referred to as 'Atomic Archie', he used his smart passing game to give shape and purpose to the teams he played in.
Archie had attended a local high school in Paisley, and signed for the local senior team St Mirren at sixteen, before moving to England, where he spent the remainder of his playing career.
Archie helped to lift the Scotland World Cup campaign from what had been a disaster, both on and off the pitch. Of that magic moment Gemmill said,
'I would have to pick my goal against Holland as the highlight of my international career. It was one of those goals you dream about. It often pops up on television all these years later and it looks better every time I see it!

What a pity we had made a mess of the previous matches in the finals'.

When Scotland played Holland in the World Cup play offs in 2003, interest in Archie's great goal was revived with contact from radio and TV companies in both Scotland and Holland wanting to have Archie recall that goal and his memories of the occasion

Before the 2002 World Cup, BBC sports online listed what they considered to be the most remarkable goals in the World Cup. Archie's goal was selected as the fifth most memorable goal, with the five goals topping the list being as follows:

1. Diego Maradona's goal when he started his run within the Argentina half of the fields against England in 1986.
2. Michael Owen's goal against Argentina in 1998.
3. A goal by the Brazilian Carlos Alberto in the 1970 final in Mexico.
4. Aric Haan's goal a 40 yard shot for Holland v Italy in 1978 which took Holland to the final.
5. Archie Gemmill's goal for Scotland against Holland in Argentina in 1978. Yes it was quite a goal and it has been described as the greatest Scottish goal ever.

At the Scottish Football Museum at Hampden Park in Glasgow, there is a special display of the Gemmill goal showing Archie's path to scoring as he weaved his way past life sized Dutch defenders. It is indeed an inspirational display.

Gemmill has recalled in detail how his goal came about.

'The ball broke to him near the right hand touch line. He then skipped past Wim Jansen (later to manage Celtic successfully), and was able to send Ruud Krol the wrong way by dummying him. Another Dutch player Jan Poortvliet, came in to tackle with a desperate lunge. Archie was able to put the ball between Jan's legs, and the goalkeeper, Jongbloed committed himself. Gemmill was able to score by shooting over the goalkeeper's head.

It is interesting that Archie only touched the ball with his left foot, which he did six times as he beat four of the players in orange and white shirts. Brian Moore the famous football commentator for ITV, described the goal as 'A Goal in a Million'.

As a result of that goal, Archie Gemmill's place in both Scottish and World Cup football has been assured. Just as his fellow Paisley 'Buddy' Archie McLean had done years before in South America, they both gave credence to the statement 'keep your eyes on Paisley', or in this case 'keep your eyes on Paisley footballers playing in South America'. David Coleman, who in 1978 was the BBC's main football commentator, made the following comment on the Gemmill goal in the World Cup game between Scotland and Holland in Argentina. 'A Brilliant Individual Goal has put Scotland in Dreamland'.

As a footnote to that goal, the Scottish Football Museum's publicity leaflet in 2006 shows on its front cover Archie Gemmill's salute after scoring that goal.

Eleven

A History of J and P Coats Ipiranga Mill in Sao Paulo

by J. S. Nisbet

As a result of contact with Coats London Office and their enquiries with Coats operation in Sao Paulo, I received the following reply.

It's amazing, we have found some notes with regards to Coats Corrente history since 1907. The history was written by John Nisbet who was the Managing Director of the Ipiranga Mill, in 1949.   Archie McLean was mentioned in this history . It went on to say that Archie was a foreman in the mill, and noted that he was one of the pioneers of football in Brazil.

J.S. Nisbet recorded, that the land was bought in 1907, in the Ipiranga district, outside the city of Sao Paulo,on which the mill now stands.   It was connected to the city by a tramway which runs from Cambuci onwards through quiet countryside. A small river, the Tamanduate, ran through the land, and provided water for bleaching and dyeing for the next 40 years. The land to the east of the river was later either sold or expropriated, and in the 1960's a main avenue was built on the west bank. Until about 1930, there was a narrow gauge decauville line from the mill to the Ipiranga station on the Sao Paulo railway, but the bridge over the Tamanduate was washed away, and the municipal authority's permission was never obtained for it to be rebuilt.

In front of the mill, where the Probel factory now stands, was the field of the Ipiranga Football Club, which played in the first league until the 1930's. The Rua do Manifesto was an unpaved road until 1946, when it was surfaced for the first time. The 'bondes' came down the Rua Sorocabanos and turned right into the Rua Silva Bueno. It was quite a convenient, fast method of travel in those days. (The word 'bond' for tramcar arose out of an association of the vehicle itself with the bond issue, which financed the road transport system).

The period of 1909 till 1920 was one of good business but with little growth. Production was almost entirely domestic sewing thread on spools. Spinning capacity was very limited, and all first quality yarns were imported. Empty spools of white wood were also imported from Finland, but spools from grumichava wood, (brown) were made at Ipiranga. Bleaching and black dyeing were done locally, but almost all coloured threads were imported.

It was not until the years 1922-1924 that the mill needed extension. Every department from spinning to spooling was enlarged, without changing the central layout or production flow. That this could be done so completely, was a great compliment to the original architects of the mill. Now spinning, twisting and finishing machinery was imported and hand dyeing boards were installed in the dye-works, which made the mill more or less self sufficient in non-fast colours.

There must have been some housing problems at this time, possibly on account of the additional number of workers needed because of the larger mill. Anyhow a 'vila operaria' was built of 51 houses in and around the Rua do Fico. In the same year 11 staff houses were built in the Rua Jorge Morreira.

The new yarn store in the north-east corner of the mill grounds, meant sacrificing the bowling green, of which the British staff were so proud. (The turf was donated to the Sao Paulo Athletic Club).

In the early 1930's, after the world slump, foreign exchange became very scarce, and for the first time, restrictions were imposed on imports of yarns. This led to the purchase of companies, which provided a source of yarn and spools for the Ipiranga mill during these years as there was never sufficient to meet demand. Management at 6,000 miles away, started issuing directives. Second and third shifts were forced on the mill before workers could be trained. The result was a crisis in 1943, when the waste figures hit the ceiling. Top management was changed (in Brazil – not where it might have been!), and a more gradual rate of growth was accepted.

In 1942 the old mill office, a humble single storey building, had to be increased to house the selling division staff, which was moved from Rio de Janeiro. It was then that the managing director took up 'residence' in Ipiranga. (From 1939 to 1942 the appointment was still held by Herbert Presyman, but he was fully occupied as naval attaché at the British Embassy in Rio).

The end of the war brought both relief and problems. Shipping was still scarce and disorganised. Supplies of yarns and spare parts were almost impossible to obtain on time. Travel improved in 1946 when the first scheduled passenger air flights were started. This coincided with a sudden rise of the Brazilian interest in industrial development and Sao Paulo city almost doubled in size in six years. It was a sellers' market, everything produced by the Ipiranga mill fell far short of the country's demand for its products.

It is difficult now to picture the mill in those days before the new mill at Vila Ema brought relief. It can easily be understood that the transfer of all spinning, winding, twisting and gassing to Vila Ema, and the opening of the new Sao Paulo depot in the Hua Silva Bueno came as a great relief. The phasing-out of the spool turning department and its eventual closure made space for the synthetic dye-works.

Even the mill entrance has changed. Until 1958, when the present façade was built; there was only an old thin metal gate, which gave neither protection nor dignity to the entrance. (It may be of interest to know that the old black man who opened this gate and swept the yard before 1939, came out to Brazil as a slave from Africa with his mother). The industrial development of Ipiranga and district caused the River Tamanduate to become polluted, and by 1946 the water supply became a major worry at the mill.

A deep well (120 Metres) was sunk at the north-west corner of the ground at Ipiranga, but it was clear from early tests that the volume of water would not be nearly enough to satisfy the needs, which at that time were about 4000 tons per day.

It was thought advisable to find an alternative site where a wet processing department could be built, if the town water supply at Ipiranga continued to fall short of needs.

After much searching, an area of land was bought on the right bank of the River Tiete near Jacarei, next to the town's water reservoir, with access to a possible effluent below the weir.

As it happened, very shortly after the purchase had been made, through the good offices of a friend in the water department, we were given a 6inch intake to replace the two existing 3inch intakes – the difference in favour of the Mill being about 200% - and from then on the water problems have really ceased to exist.

The Company was fortunate that the water supply improved when it did, because it helped the transfer of trade of handicrafts from Paisley to Brazil. From 1952, imports had become more and more difficult, and in 1954, a last licence was given on the condition that arrangements would be made to manufacture these articles locally. The Mill had already received supplies of improved cotton from Sao Miguel and were importing additional dyeing, mercerising and finishing machinery. The trade mark owners had some doubts about authorising the use of the Anchor mark for the local production, but did so after seeing samples. Pearl Cotton, Stranded Cotton and Floss Embroidery, in that order, were introduced, and their acceptance exceeded their most optimistic hopes. By 1956 the transfer of trade was complete. The quality fell short of articles made with Egyptian cotton, but has proved acceptable for the Brazilian market. The standard of dyeing was as good as that of the imported articles, again, the lustre was slightly disappointing.

The central strike in Sao Paulo in October 1957 was an historic event in the history of the Ipiranga mill. The labour union intimidated the workers at the mill, and forced them to strike in sympathy with the other factories in the city.

The government was very weak, and the strikers were actually led in their marches through the streets by the Vice-Governor of the State. However after a few days, the Forca Publica was ordered out to maintain law and order. The factory was called by phone to enquire as to whether the Iparanga mill was prepared to house a "small detachment of police", and to serve as the local base for the garrison of the Forca Publica in the district of Ipiranga.

The suggestion was accepted with enthusiasm, although the company could hardly have done otherwise. That night, about 11oclock, a column of infantry, cavalry, staff cars and radio vehicles, numbering in all about 200 persons and 20 horses, arrived at the mill and asked for accommodation. Fortunately at this time, the new dining hall was weather proof although far from being finished. The men were able to doss down for the night, and the next day we arranged mattresses for them. The officers used the board room as their bedroom.

After a few days, the factory got to know the visitors very well. The officers were very "simpaticos" and very helpful. Within a matter of hours after their arrival, the mill was working again. The relations between the girl workers and the soldiers were excellent.

When the strike was eventually broken and the detachment received orders to leave, there was a "march past" at the gate when the colonel took the salute, and the directors of the company stood by his side.

The final episode was a cocktail party given for the officers in the sports club behind the depot. It was an event never to be forgotten. The sight of the officers of the Forca Publica dancing the eightsome reel was perhaps the highlight!

Management at the Mill
Prior to 1939

General Managers:	R.S.McNicol
	S.S.McCulloch
	William Steel
	Harold Windsor
Spinning:	Frank Wooley
	Sam Brown
	Eddie Southern
Twisting:	A.D.Hutchison
	William Kerr
	Jack Hunter
Polishing:	J.M. Love
	Jack Hunter
Dyeing:	W.C.Mair
	Herbert Wright
	James Hogg
Finishing:	R.Gemmel
	Robert Rankin

Engineers:	Alex Rowand
	R.Kerr
	Ben Thompson
	Bob Bissett
	Stanley Gibson

Administration (Heads): C.J.Allwood (1909-1944)
J.G. Hamilton (1911)

Assistants:	George O'May
	William Harrison
	Jock Barr
	William Bilsland
	J.S. Nisbet

Foreman Tenters:	Archie McLean
	William Waddall
	Edward Markison
	Hector McNeil
	Thomas Ferguson

After 1945

General Managers:	Ted Combes
	George Dinwiddie
	Jim Cowan
	Norman Munro
	Tom Affleck

Spinning:	Sam Brown
	Gavin Black

Twisting:	Fred Rastall
	Charles Vines
	Jack Manwell
Polishing:	Jack Tipple
Dyeing:	James Hogg
	John Stevens
	George Thomson
Finishing:	Alex Rowand
	Tom Affleck
Engineers:	Stanley Gibson
	Andrew Johnston
	Ken McLellan
	David Hamilton
	John Crawford
	E.Halfpenny
Standards:	Stanley Durrell
	Murray Jackson
Foreman Tenters:	Colin Brown
	Bob Milne
	William Chittick

By the early 1950's it was possible to replace these experts by locally trained staff, but until then the control of lengths and appearance of the finished articles largely depended on their personal skills.

Twelve
To Play For Fun or Pay

After the exit of England from the World Cup in Germany in July 2006, the English press were unhappy with the efforts of the highly paid members of the England football team.

At this time, a book was published written by Mike Collins entitled 'All Round Genius: The unknown story of Britain's Greatest Sportsman', about all round sportsman Max Woosnam. In the Daily Mail on Thursday July 27th 2006, David Thomas asked the question "Was he the greatest sportsman of all time?" Thomas outlined some of Max Woosnam's achievements.

'In his prime Woosnam – who smoked Capstan full strength cigarettes all his adult life, won the Olympic gold and silver medals, plus a Wimbledon title. He was Captain of England's amateur and professional football teams, he played golf off a scratch handicap, and he scored the perfect break at snooker.

He was also a successful businessman and a war hero, a man who knew, as modern athletes do not, the difference between sporting conflict and the real thing.

However, there was nothing dour or gloomy about Woosnam. He relished any challenge, whether crunching into a tackle on the football field, or playing Charlie Chaplin at table tennis, using only a butter knife.

In 1919, Woosnam joined Manchester city, still playing as an amateur. He was so good, he was invited to captain Great Britain's team at the 1920 Antwerp

Olympics. Sadly, he was forced to decline as he had already been selected for the British Tennis Squad. Woosnam and his partner Noel Turnball, won a gold medal in the men's doubles, beating a Japanese pair called Kumagae and Kashio. 'Woosnam's low volleys and service returns were the deciding factor' reported the magazine Lawn Tennis and Badminton.

Having won gold in the morning, Woosnam went out to play another final, partnering Kitty McKane in the mixed doubles. Fatigued by his earlier efforts, Woosnam took only a silver medal this time.

In the following year, Woosnam played a full season for Manchester City, during which time he was appointed Captain. He also captained England's amateur football team, leading the full England side in a 1 – 0 win against Wales.

When the football season ended, he picked up his tennis racket again, popping down to Wimbledon, where he won the mixed doubles title. He sailed to America, where he captained Great Britain in the Davis Cup. The cup was played on continuous tournament. Unfortunately, the British were knocked out by Australia in the second round.

It was now early August, and as their ship was not due for another month, Woosnam played a series of golf matches against prominent Americans, winning every time.

The English press indicated that had those highly paid professionals of the England football team extended themselves as Max Woosnam had done, they would have progressed further in the World Cup.

Indeed Max's achievements were exceptional and

never likely to be repeated. Today's players are trained physically to a high level, and are encouraged to develop skills relating to a particular sport.

There is the case of Andy Goram who while a player in the goals for Glasgow Rangers, wanted to spend the summer playing cricket. Andy was an accomplished cricketer, having played for Scotland. The Rangers management team were unhappy with Goram's involvement, as they feared any injury would have robbed them of a player in the coming season. They did all they could to prevent Andy playing.

Lawrie Reilly was born in 1928, and spent all his football career at Hibernian. He was the centre forward of the 'famous five' forward line. During Reilly's time at Hibs, they won the league championship on four occasions, and became the first British team to play in the European cup. Over a nine year period, Reilly played 38 times for Scotland and scored 23 goals, including 7 against England. In November 2005, Lawrie became inducted into The Hall of Fame at the Scottish Football Museum.

Lawrie Reilly is unimpressed by the inflated salaries of the football players in the twenty first century. Reilly tells that when he played for Hibs, the average home gate was 30,000 and he was paid £16 per week. He played at Wembley against England on five occasions and he scored in four of them but was paid no more than £30 a game. Reilly, a survivor from the fifties, has concerns about rates of pay, and players today being paid £100,000 plus per week. Laurie worked as a painter to trade, and on a Saturday he would work from 8.00 a.m. till noon at his trade, before reporting to Easter Road for the 3.00 p.m. Saturday kick off for the home games. He goes on to state that he feels the game has lost a lot of the atmosphere it had when fans would stand on the terracing rather than sit. He realises times have changed, but feels as he always did, that football must entertain the spectators, and players must demonstrate skills and abilities which will endear them to the fans just as he did in the fifties.

As the game developed later in Brazil, than in England, the debate on paying players came to the fore, and those who wanted to pay players won out. A number of teams in the Northern part of England relied on Scottish players who brought their passing style to the English game. The Scots did not have private incomes, and needed to be rewarded for their play, and initially they would receive 'under the counter' payments.

The English Football Association, who refer to themselves as the FA became aware of these developments, and they were not happy about the idea of professionalism. However at the beginning of the 1885 season, payments to players became officially part of the English game. The season 1888 – 89 saw Preston North End win the league without losing a game, and then failed to score on one occasion. The Preston team of that season had eight Scots on their team, all being paid for their services.

In Scotland, there was similar conflict, although a prominent team Queen's Park was amateur. When the FA Cup competition began, Queen's Park entered the competition, as they felt there was not a challenge in Scotland at the time for them to meet. In the season 1890-

91 the Scottish league was formed with eleven teams; however Queens Park was not part of the league.

Just as the FA had concerns with professionalism, so did the Scottish FA. In the first season, Renton were expelled for playing a team, Edinburgh Saints, who were deemed to be professionals. The Scottish FA began to realise, that the Scottish game would lose their best players to the Northern teams in England who had more money to pay players. So in 1893 they agreed to legalise the payment to players.

The debate on professionalism raged in Sao Paulo, where those with the background Charles Miller had, could afford to play for the fun of it, but there were those such as Archie McLean, working class players, who although they were not professional, did receive some reimbursement for the entertainment they provided. Just as in Scotland and England, many of the players who were not in jobs which allowed them to enjoy the opportunity to play for fun, needed to be paid for their time as they played football, so it was in Brazil.

The Gentleman V the Players was a matter for discussion and debate at the end of the Nineteenth Century, in Brazil. Those who were leading lights in Football Associations in Brazil mainly did so because they could afford to. They were not poor or from deprived backgrounds nor were they employed to work in the mills or factories where they would suffer a loss of earnings, an essential part of the family income, if they took time out to play football. The day was soon to come, when the majority of those who played would be paid to do so .

So it was that as the twentieth century emerged, so did the

professional football player in many parts of the world, with the pros and cons this brought to the beautiful game and in ways which would tarnish the image of football.

Appendices

Appendix One

Letter written by Charles Miller, published in the Banister Court School Magazine when Charles was in England, he attended Banister Court School in Southampton.

1) From volume. III. No 31, March 1904 of the Bannister Court School Magazine

"S. Paul's Town (sic) is, situated about fifty miles west of the seaport of Santos, and 3,000 feet above sea level of Santos. The railway between Santos and S.Paul's belongs to an English company, and is managed by Englishmen, and it is one of the best organised and kept roads in the world. The trains leave Santos and run on level ground for about fifteen miles, then are pulled up the side of a mountain or serra for seven miles to the height of 3,000 feet, and then on level ground to S.Paul's. The pulling of the trains up and down the serra is worked by endless cables on the grip system. The present population of

S.Paul's is anything between 280,000 and 300,000 inhabitants, the greater part being Italians. The whole town has a European appearance. Electric-cars or trams run all through the town and out into the suburbs, six miles or more. The force for the electric power is supplied by a large waterfall fifteen miles out of town; nearly all the factories are worked by electricity from the same fall. The centre streets of the town are paved with wooden blocks, the same as the High Street in Southampton. The climate is very much as in England, very changeable. For instance, it ought to be pretty hot now, being midsummer, but for the last week the thermometer has not been over 73 degrees F, not even summer heat."
(Source ' An Entirely Different Game')

Appendix Two
Goals and games by Charles Miller, his championship winning seasons in Brazil
1902

8 May	SPAC v Paulistano	4-0	1 Goal
13 May	SPAC v MacKenzie College	3-0	1 Goal
8 June	SPAC v Internacional	3-0	1 Goal
29 June	SPAC v Paulistano	0-1	
20 July	SPAC v Germania	4-0	2 Goals
3 Aug.	SPAC v Germania	3-0	1 Goal
24 Aug.	SPAC v Internacional	0-0	
20 Sept.	SPAC v MacKenzie College	4-4	2 Goals
26 Oct.	SPAC v Paulistano	2-1	2 Goals

1903

21 May	SPAC v MacKenzie College	2-0	1 Goal
24 June	SPAC v Paulistano*	0-2	
5 July	SPAC v Internacional	5-0	
19 July	SPAC v Germania	4-1	1 Goal
2 Aug.	SPAC v Paulistano*	4-0	(Scorers not named)
9 August	SPAC v Germania	1-1	1 Goal
27 Sept.	SPAC v Internacional	3-0	
25 Oct.	SPAC v Paulistano	2-1	

1904

12 June	SPAC v Germania	1-0	1 Goal
19 June	SPAC v Paulistano	1-1	1 Goal
29 June	SPAC v AA das Palmeiras	5-0	1 Goal
10 July	SPAC v Germania	3-2	1 Goal

24 July	SPAC v Paulistano*	0-0	
31 July	SPAC v AA das Palmeiras*3-0		
		(scorers not named)	
7 Aug.	SPAC v Internacional	5-0	1 Goal
15 Aug.	SPAC v MacKenzie College	1-0	1 Goal
18 Sept.	SPAC v Internacional	4-1	1 Goal
28 Sept.	SPAC v MacKenzie College 5-0		
		(2 goals unattributed)	
30 Oct.	SPAC v Paulistano	1-0	1 Goal

* Miller's name appears in the SPAC line-up on the day of the game, but not in the match report.
(Source 'O Estado de Sao Paulo')

Appendix Three
Teams Archie McLean Lined up with : 1912 – 1918
Season 1912
Archie lined up for Sao Paulo A.C.

The line up included:

> Delghton, Morrow, Winyard, Whitworth,
> Hammond, Pitt, Hutchinson, Boyes, Bradshaw,
> Smith, Banks, Colston, Embleton, Pegler,
> Hamilton, Bradfield, Roberts, MacLean

The Teams in the League were:

> Americano
> Paulistano
> Mackenzie
> Germania
> Sao Paulo
> Internacional
> Ipiranga

And Sao Paulo A.C. finished 5th.

Season 1913
Archie lined up for Americano

The line up included:

> Hugo, Menezes Hoopton; Bertone II, Bertone I
> Sebastiao; Irineu, Decio, Mauricio, Alencar, MacLean

The Teams in the League were

> Americano
> Internacional
> Ipiranga
> Germania
> Corinthians
> Santos - and Amerciano finished 1st

Season 1914

Archie Lined up for Wanderers

The line up included:

Hutchinson, Pegler Witworth; Breakley, Allwood
Bradshaw; Banks, Bradfield, Campbell, MacLean
Hopkins

The Teams in the League were

Sao Bento

Paulistano

Mackenzie

Ipiranga

Wanderers

Palmeiras

And Wanderers Finished 5th

Season 1915

Archie Lined up for Wanderers

The Line up included:

Smith, Gino, Pegler; Felicio, Police, Bradfield
Humberton, Scott, Felix, MacLean, Hopkins

The Team in the League were

Palmeiras

Mackenzie

Ipiranga

Paulistano

Wanderers

Sao Bento

And Wanderers Finished 5th

Season 1916

Archie lined up for Sao Bento

The line up included:

Orlando Penteado, Zacharias R Burgos;
Bucker, Lagreca, Moraes; Damaso, J Pedro,
Irineu, MacLean, Hopkins

The Team in the League were

Paulistano

Sao Bento

Mackenzie

Ipiranga

Santos

Palmeiras

Palestra

And Sao Bento finished 2nd

Season 1917

Archie Lines up for Sao Bento

The Line up Included

Hugo, Menezes, Paulino; Zaca, Lagreca, Bartho
Mimi, Dias, Alencar, MacLean, Bucker

The Teams in the League were:

Paulistano

Palestra

Corinthians

Santos

Palmeiras

Ipiranga

Sao Bento

International

Mackenzie - and Sao Bento finished 7th

Season 1918

Archie Lined up for Sao Bento

The Line up included:

      Horacio, Bertone, Bartho; Bertone II,
      Lagreca, Jose Franco; Zucchi, Dias
      Collo, MacLean, Infantini

TheTeams in the League were:

      Paulistano
      Corinthians
      Palmeiras
      Santos
      Ipiranga
      Sao Bento
      Minas Gerais
      Internacional
      Mackenzie
      Palestra Italia

And Sao Bento finished 6th

(Source '0 Caminho da Bola 1902 – 1952')

Appendix Four
Interstate Game

Inter-state games played by Archibald McLean for the Paulista XI against Rio de Janeiro

1 – First game – 28 June 1914

Played in Rio de Janeiro – Paulista 4 x 2 Rio de Janeiro

Paulista XI line-up: Morais; Orlando & O'May; Gulo, Rubens Salles and Freidenreich; Formiga, Juvenal, Decio, McLean and Hopkins.

2 – Second game – 1915

Played in Sao Paulo – Paulistas 2 x 1 Rio de Janeiro

Paulista XI: Casimiro; Morelli and Osni; Lagreca, Bianco and Egidio; Formiga, Demonstenes, Nazareth, McLean and Hopkins

3 – Third game – 191 5 – Another game this time in Rio de Janeiro, with a victory for the locals by 5 x 2. Hopkins scored one of the Paulista goals. Paulista XI: Casimiro; Morelli and Osny; Lagreca, Rubens Salles and Egidio; Formiga, Demosthenes, Na\areth, Mcleena and Hopkins.

4 – Fourth game – 1915 in Sao Paulo and the Paulistas smashed the Rio de Janeiro team by 8 x 0. McLean scored 1 goal.

Paulista XI: Casimiro; Morelli and Osny; Galo, Rubens Salles and Lagreca; Formiga, Demosthenes, Friedenrecih, McLean and Hopkins.

Final quote taken from page 114 –

"1917 saw the uprise of several young local good players, and it was thus that the Paulista XI was renovated, and unfortunately no more would players such as McLean and Hopkins be seen.' (Source 'History of Football in Brazil')

Appendix Five

LIGA PAULISTA

This appendix shows details of the teams in the LIGA PAULISTA – the Sao Paulo Football League. The first fixture was played on 3 May 1902, and there were 5 teams in the league.

Team	Nationality of Players/	Team Leader
Sao Paulo Athletics Club	British	Charles Miller
MacKenzie College	Americans	Augustus Shaw
Sport Club Int'national	Various	Antonia Casiminro de Costa
Sport Club Germania	German	Hans Nobling
CAP	Brazilian	Group of Young Brazilians

(Club Athletico Paulistano   )
(Source 'God is Brazillian')

Appendix Six

2-3-5 Formation

The formation of teams at the early part of the twentieth century was a 2-3-5 set up as shown below.

Goalkeeper

Right Back   **Left Back**

Right Half   **Centre Half**   **Left Half**

Rt Wing / Inside Rt/Centre Forward / Inside Left /Left Wing

To illustrate this formation the Scottish Wanderers for their first game on August 1912 against SC International's Extra Team. The 2-3-5 line up was

Gardner

Clark   Hamilton

Parker   Richardson   Kennedy

Woolley   Wright   McLean   Simpson   Hamilton

The team had Archie McLean at centre forward. The team all worked in Coats Sao Paulo Mill, and the names look as if the team was all Scottish.

The 4-3-3 or 4-4-2 Formation

When Alf Ramsey retired from playing as a right back, he took up the job as manager of Ipswich Town. Within the space of few seasons, he had won Ipswich promotion twice to the first Division, (now the Premiership). Edinburgh born Jimmy Leadbetter arrived at Portman Road, the home of Ipswich just before Alf. He joined from Brighton for

£1750 as a left wing, and he was part of the success the team had in reaching the First Division.

Alf Ramsey realised his team were no competition for the big guns of their new league unless something radical changed in the tactics his team employed.

The plan was to have Jimmy Leadbetter stay deep and to find the team's strikers, Ray Crawford and Ted Philips, or the right winger Roy Stephenson with passes, and to forget about the way he used to play as a conventional left winger. Alf Ramsey's thoughts were to play Leadbetter as part of 4-3-3 format in midfield, and to leave the right back, (Alf's own position)with no-one to play against. Praising Leadbetter, Alf Ramsey stated 'Jimmy was very, very good at doing what he was told'.

In recent times, managers particularly when playing away from home, have adopted formations such as

4 - 5 - 1 or 3 - 5 - 1 - 1

In both cases teams play with just one striker and rely on counter attacking play to score goals.

The two men went their separate ways: Alf Ramsey to manage England to glory in 1966 and to a knighthood; Jimmy Leadbetter to sell newspapers outside the ground at Ipswich to help him make ends meet. Jimmy had convinced Alf to play without the conventional wingers, and it is not too fanciful to say 'Jimmy Leadbetter was the Scot who helped England to their 1966 World Cup triumph'.

In the final against West Germany the England line up was a 4-4-2 format.

Banks

Cohen	Charlton (J)	Moore	Wilson
Ball	Stiles	Charlton (R)	Peters
	Hunt	Hurst	

In contract West Germany lined up with a 4-3-3 formation.

(Source 'McFootball')

Appendix Seven
The Old Pele
Arthur (Artur) Friedenreich

Artur's father was a German businessman, and his mother was an Afro-Brazilian. At the time Artur started to play football, the game was then played by the upper classes. Friedenreich had to pretend to be a white man with an all the year round tan.

Artur took thirty minutes to sort his hair before each game, using Brilliantine to straighten his hair flat into his scalp. He made his debut for Germania, and later moved to a Sao Paulo team called Paulistano, which is now defunct. He finished top scorer for 17 years in the Sao Paulo League. (Not even Pele achieved this feat).

Artur was the first Brazilian star, and he played in the Samba Style.

The peak of his career was to score the only goal against Uruguay in the 1919 Copa America Final. The day after this game, Artur's boot, which scored the winning goal, was displayed in a downtown jewellers in Rio.

In 1921, the Copa America was held in Argentina, which was considered to be the wealthiest country in South America. Artur, in his twenty ninth year, was very upset when he was not selected to play for Brazil. In spite of this age discrimination, Artur played in endless lucrative friendlies. Brazil continued to cling onto its amateur status till 1918. Artur used this income to live an extravagant lifestyle. Sadly, Friedenreich's family threw out his goal scoring records onto a Sao Paulo rubbish heap.

Eventually Artur's hair, after years of treatment, had

become straight. When he died in 1969, for Artur, senility had set in, so he had forgotten both his name and his time as a footballer.
(Source 'Cult Football')

Appendix Eight
Roll Of Honour

The Scottish Football Association (SFA) have instituted an international roll of honour, so when a Scottish footballer has played for the National Team on fifty occasions, the player is appointed to the international roll of honour. The player becomes the subject of a specially commissioned painting and receives a gold medal.

For a player in the national team in 1902, there were three opportunities to pull on a Scotland shirt in games against

1 Ireland at Grovenor Park in Ireland
2 Wales at Capplelow (The home of Greenock Morton)
3 England at Ibrox

Which was the home international's competition.

In 2002, a player established in the national team had the chance to play in nine internationals for Scotland.

1 France in Paris
2 Nigeria at Pittodrie (Aberdeen's home ground)
3 South Korea in Busan
4 South Africa in Hong Kong
5 Denmark in Hampden Park
6 Faroe Islands at Tofitir
7 Iceland in Reykjavik
8 Canada at Easter Road (Hibs Home ground)
9 Portugal at Braga

It is really just in the modern era, that players have received 50 or more caps, with George Young of Rangers, who played for Scotland from 1946 to 1957 and won 53 caps, being the first to enter the Roll of Honour.

As at the 6th September 2006, the players on the roll of

honour are:

The main club(s) played are in brackets

ROLL OF HONOUR

	Caps
Kenny Dalglish (1971-1986)(Celtic &Liverpool)	102
Jim Leighton (1982-1998) (Aberdeen)	91
Alex McLeish (1980-1993)(Aberdeen)	77
Paul McStay (1983-1997) (Celtic)	76
Tom Boyd (1990-2001)Motherwell & Celtic)	72
Willie Miller (1975-1989)(Aberdeen)	65
Christian Dailly (1997 to date)(Blackburn Rovers & West Ham United)	62
Danny McGrain (1973-1982)(Celtic)	62
Richard Gough (1983-1993) (Rangers)	61
Ally McCoist (1985-1998)(Rangers)	61
John Collins (1988-1999) (Hibernian & Celtic)	58
Roy Aitken (1979-1991)(Celtic)	57
Gary McAllister (1990-1999)(Leeds United & Coventry City)	57
Denis Law (1958-1974)(Manchester United)	55
Maurice Malpas (1984-1992)(Dundee United)	55
Billy Bremner (1965-1975)(Leeds United)	54
Graeme Souness (1974-1986) (Liverpool)	54
George Young (1946-1957) (Rangers) ...	53
Alan Rough (1976-1986)(Partick Thistle)	53
Kevin Gallacher (1988-2001)(Dundee United & Blackburn Rovers)	53
Joe Jordan (1973-1982) (Leeds United & Manchester United)	52

Colin Hendry (1993-2001)(Dundee & Blackburn Rovers)	51
Asa Hartford (1972-1982)(Manchester City & Nottingham Forest)	50
Gordon Strachan (1980-1992)(Aberdeen and Manchester United)	50

David Weir (Hearts, Everton and Rangers) became the 25th player to join this select group on 6th September 2006. Up till 1976, the rule the SFA had was that players could only be awarded a cap, when the game was against Northern Ireland, Wales or England, and only one cap was awarded per season, not one for each match.

Eddie Turnball who played for Hibs and later was manager for Hibs and Aberdeen, played for Scotland but only against European teams such as Belgium, Switzerland, France and Austria. Finally in the 1958 World Cup final in Sweden, Eddie played 3 games. However Eddie Turnball was never awarded a Scottish Cap.

Eddie had the distinction of being the first British player to score a goal in a European competition, Hibs being the first team to play in Europe.

After a lot of lobbying by Eddie's friends, in the spring of 2006, the SFA Board decided to award commemorative caps to players who had played for Scotland but had not received a cap. Eddie Turnball was invited to attend the next international match Scotland would play at Hampden. This match was a friendly against Switzerland on March 1 2006, an evening match. At half time Eddie was presented with a Cap in a symbolic ceremony. It was a cold evening, and Scotland lost the match, but the 82year old Eddie

Turnbull was now over the moon at finally receiving his Scotland Cap.
(Source: 'Scottish Football Museum')

Appendix Nine

THE PACAEMBU STADIUM

In 1926, the city of Sao Paulo gave land to the state, in order to build a stadium in the district of Pacaembu, which was situated in a pleasant area of the City .The stadium was inaugurated by the President of , Brazil, Getulio Vargas and the Mayor Adhemar de Barros April 27, 1940 at 10.00am in front of 60.000 people. It was regarded as the most modern and largest stadium in South America with a capacity of approximately 70.000 spectators. The record attendance was recorded in 1942, during a Paulista Derby between Sao Paulo and Corinthians, which was a three each goal draw. In 1970 the stadium's capacity was increased by 15.000. The stadium now accommodates 71,281 spectators. In 1961, the stadium was renamed the Municipal Stade Paulo Machado de Carvalho, in homage to the man who was responsible for the 1958 World Cup successful win in Sweden. Paulists consider the Pacaembu an inheritance from the city, which has meant that the municipal council has never sold the stadium. It is one of the most complete stadiums in Brazil, since in addition to accommodating Corinthians games, it has excellent facilities for other sports including swimming, boxing, volleyball and tennis. Pacaembu Stadium is one of the most beautifully located stadiums in the world. It is in the Pacaembu valley, near the centre of town, in a very nice neighbourhood – Pacaembu – of Sao Paulo City. The architects used the slopes of the valley for the stands on both sides. Neither Charles Miller or Archie McLean ever played there, they only went as spectators.

Several games of the World Cup 1950 were played in this stadium, plus other international competitions. Before the building of the Morumbi Stadium, owned by Sao Paulo Futebol Clube, in the 60s, it was considered this city's Wembley.

The park, or esplanade, outside the main entrance is called "Praca Charles Miller", after he who is considered the "Father of Brazilian Football".

The stadium belongs to the City Hall of Sao Paulo, but historically and romantically, all the supporters of Corinthians Paulista feel it is theirs, as they feel perfectly at home there. Most Brazilian and Paulista league games are played in this stadium, plus occasional musical shows. (Sources : Nicholas Savage and John Mills)

APPENDIX TEN

THE FAMOUS BRAZILIAN FOOTBALL STRIP

In 1953, a nineteen year old named Aldyr Garcia Schlee set about to design the Brazilian football strip. He produced four designs based on famous Brazilian footballers of the early 1950s.

The first design Aldyr produced was based on Claudio, who played in the right wing for Corinthians.

The second design he made was based on Pinheird, a Fluminense defender, and of this design Schlee commented at the time that it was really a windcheater with a yellow bold tick around the waist.

The third design showed Ademir Meneses of Vasco in a green and yellow striped shirt. Meneses scored nine goals in the 1950 World Cup, which is still a record for Brazil.

The final design showed Baltazar who was known as 'The Little Golden Head', as he had scored many outstanding headed goals.

Having made the four designs, Aldyr decided which combinations he felt would be the best to produce a football strip the Brazilian nation would be proud of. When he had made a decision as to what the strip should look like, he painted the strip in much more detail and added a background of the Maracana Stadium. He submitted the finalised design to the Brazilian Sports Confederation for their consideration.

The rest is history, in that Brazil have played with distinction in their distinctive strip of yellow and green

stripes and cobalt blue for the past fifty years.
(Source Futebol: The Brazilian Way of Life)

Bibliography

1   Bellos, Alex
Futebol – The Brazilian Way of Life
Bloomsbury, London, 2002
2   Cairney, John
A Scottish Football Hall of Fame
Mainstream, Edinburgh 2004
3.   Castro, Ruy
Garrincha
The Triumph and Tragedy of
Brazilian's Forgotten Football
Held Yellow Jersey Press, London 2004
4.   Galvin, Robert
Football's Greatest Heroes
The National Football Museum
Hall of Fame
Robson Books
5.   Gemmill, Archie
My Autobiography
Both Sides of the Border
Hodder and Stoughton, London 2005
6.   Giller, Norman
McFootball
The Scottish Heroes of the English Game
Robson Books, London 2003
7.   Goldblats, David
Football Yearbook 2004/5
Dorling Kindersley

8.   Harris, Harry
Pele, His Life and Times
Robson Books, London, 2001
9.   Hunt, Chris
The History of the Fifa World Cup
World Cup Stories
Interact, Ware 2006
10. Hamilton, Aidan
An Entirely Different Game
The British Influence on Brazilian Football
Mainstream, Edinburgh, 1998
11. Insight Guides
Brazil
Apa Publications, London 2005
12. Jenkins, Garry
The Beautiful Team
In Search of Pele and the 1970 Brazilians
Simon and Schuster, London 1998
13. Lacey, Josh
God is Brazilian
Charles Miller, The Man Who Brought Football to Brazil
Tempus, Stroud, 2005
14. MacPherson, Archie
Flower of Scotland
A Scottish Football Odyssey
Highdown, Newbury 2005

15. Nicol, N (Compiler)
The Scottish Football League
Past Members, Part Three
Davidson, Renfrew 1994
16. Pele and Robert Fish
My Life and the Beautiful Game
New English Library 1997
17. *Pele*
The Autobiography
Simon and Schuster, London 2006
18. Potter, David
Wizards and Bravehearts
A History of the Scottish National Side
Tempus, Stroud, 2004
19. *O Caminho Da Bola 1902-1952*
1 Volume
Anos Paulistao
20. *Six Cord Thread*
The Story of Coats and Clarks
Paisley Threadmills
Paisley, 1995
21. Taylor, Chris
The Beautiful Game 1998
22. *The Rough Guide to Cult Football*
Rough Guides